Carlo Gung

Sergio Los

CARLO SCARPA

1906–1978

A Poet of Architecture

TASCHEN

HONG KONG KÖLN LONDON LOS ANGELES MADRID PARIS TOKYO

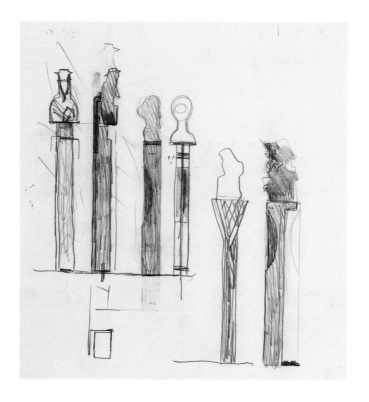

Photo page 2 ▶ Carlo Scarpa in Venice, 1976
Illustration page 4 ▶ Designs for a pedestal for a
statue of Saint Catherine in the restored Castelvecchio, Verona, 1962–1964; the drawings depict
the statue and its presentation.

© 2009 TASCHEN GmbH
Hohenzollernring 53, D-50672 Köln
www.taschen.com

Editor ▶ Peter Gössel, Bremen
Project management ▶ Swantje Schmidt, Bremen
Design and layout ▶ Gössel und Partner, Bremen
Text edited by ▶ Avinus, Berlin
Translation ▶ John S. Scott, Garmisch-Parten-
kirchen and Maureen Roycroft Sommer, Bergisch
Gladbach

Printed in Germany
ISBN: 978-3-8365-0728-8

To stay informed about upcoming TASCHEN
titles, please request our magazine at
www.taschen.com/magazine or write to
TASCHEN America, 6671 Sunset Boulevard, Suite
1508, USA-Los Angeles, CA 90028, contact-
us@taschen.com, Fax: +1-323-463.4442. We will
be happy to send you a free copy of our magazine
which is filled with information about all of our
books.

Contents

Introduction

When I think of Carlo Scarpa as a teacher, the first thing I remember is that he was a rather shadowy figure in the department. His presence was always felt, but he was seldom to be seen. He taught architectural drawing, and any classes with him had to be arranged by phone at either his office or his home. He had few students, so I was able to spend whole afternoons alone with him. As time went by, I came to realize that he had a very idiosyncratic manner of drawing, one that no longer had anything to do with the simple utilitarian presentation of existing or projected buildings. His teaching aimed at a form of drawing intended as thought. Thus, drawings for him were creative reflections, deliberations that were intended to help explain something, or arguments that could be either right or wrong and, therefore, they were far more than merely realistic depictions.

I grew up in Marostica, near Vicenza, and played as a child inside the castle walls, among the farmhouse porticos and on terraces held up by dry-stone walls, typical of areas of hillside cultivation, amidst a maze of vineyards and river embankments crisscrossed by trampled paths. I have always felt very drawn to buildings of this kind, half structure and half landscape. At that time (i.e. in the 1950s) the American architect Frank Lloyd Wright was, in my opinion, the architect whose work most closely reflected this interplay of building and natural environment. It seemed to me that he translated my own, more intuitive approach towards human efforts of design into architecture.

When I arrived in Venice with a desire to learn to build such structures, Scarpa seemed to be the architect whose works came closest to Wright's. While attending two courses on interior design and architectural representation, I realized that for me Scarpa was far more than just an imparter of Wright's ideas. I realized that the connection between architecture and context is highly complex and that first and foremost the relationship with other buildings was of prime importance. I saw that behind the most remote buildings there is always a town with a story to tell. After attending these two courses I resolved that on completing my studies I would try to join Scarpa's team.

The Context

Who was Scarpa at that time? In what context had he developed his architecture? He had studied at the Academy of Fine Arts in Venice during the transition from Classicism to Secession. The exemplary work of Otto Wagner, the doyen of the Viennese school, drew Scarpa's attention to Josef Hoffmann and Charles Rennie Mackintosh, who each paid particular attention to tectonics, craftsmanship and material in their approach. Scarpa repeatedly mentioned that during his time at the Academy, more than at the Department of Architecture, a craft atmosphere prevailed that was reminiscent of a building site.

It should be mentioned that unlike other contemporary architects, such as Ludwig Mies van der Rohe, Scarpa came to modern architecture via the Secession—the movement known in the English-speaking world as Art nouveau—and not via Neoclassicism. This point of departure was decisive for the evolution of that particular

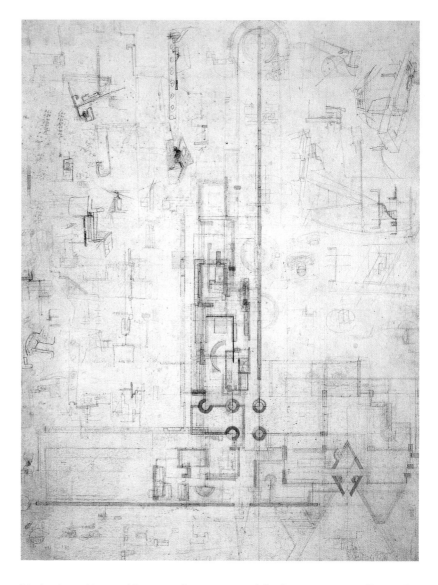

Villa Zoppas, Conegliano, Treviso, 1953
Drawing of the floor plan

Modernist architectural language that Scarpa used for the composition of his works, one that was—despite his love of classical architecture—neither rationalistic, nor neo-classical, nor minimalistic.

The ideas pursued in enlightened Modernist works ranging from Claude-Nicolas Ledoux's to le Corbusier's dissociated architectural design from the constructive-craft tradition that had linked architecture to the other visual arts. The distinction between the project and the actual building made it possible to produce drawings able to depict not only facts, but also desires, that not only related the present or the past, but also the future. Drawing became the common "writing" of a "figurative language" of form in the early Renaissance, which embraced painting, sculpture and architecture as well. In my opinion, all attempts to separate architecture from the other visual arts and raise it to the status of an independent discipline lead only to design becoming a matter of calculation and technical craftsmanship instead of art. Pictorial thinking, thinking in images, which distinguishes Scarpa's approach, is part of a tradition which goes beyond the handicraft and even withstands the mathematical approach of engineers.

Scarpa said "I draw because I want to see". This shows the extent to which seeing had a connection to knowing and constructing in his mind. It means that an architectural design proceeds from this differentiation between drawing and construction, which makes craft skills a topic of debate while preventing a descent to mere calculation, which came in with the architecture of the Enlightenment when architectural treatises became nothing but technical manuals and the first engineering schools were founded.

Scarpa always distanced himself from the functionalist as well as the historical schematism of the modern school. His feeling for learning by doing prevented him from succumbing to the abstract nature of their block diagrams, which came to replace the distributive characteristics of particular types, thereby developing a geometrically abstract system that took precedence over architecture. On the other hand, his profound historical knowledge enabled him to avoid both stylistically vague illustrations as well as the search for a progressiveness intended to legitimize the overthrow of natural architectural language. His sensibility, which was informed by cultural knowledge, is above all suspicion of being based solely on the experience of perception. The complexity of his outlook, where one image refers always to another (and consequently, like words, to meaning), does not allow one to attribute it to the psychology of visual perception. Scarpa's ability to re-work the figures he drew according to this pictorial logic, based on a profound knowledge of traditional forms, which supplied him with the criteria of selection and evaluation, is essentially a kind of "symbolic" competence. This is the sort of competence that was developed and theoretically formulated by the painters and architects of the early Renaissance, but which later came to be regarded as mere theatricality, after it was superseded by the scientific idea of objectivity.

As the system of classical Baroque architecture gave way to that of the Secession, there was a gradual transition from figure to form. If one studies the transition from the late Baroque to the "pavilion system" that was considered by Sigfried Giedion and Emil Kaufmann to identify the architecture of the Enlightenment, one is able to comprehend what made Scarpa unique. Scarpa never adopted the analytical vocabulary of architecture that is based on a juxtaposition of geometrically defined volumes. His development led him to a Neoplasticist decomposition of space without ever having evolved through Neoclassicism. Through his figures he gradually achieved a transition to the pure forms of modern abstraction.

Scarpa's first drawings—apart from the studies he completed while still at the Academy—were explorations in Neoplasticism as derived from Frank Lloyd Wright's Prairie houses and predated its specific European codification as furthered by De Stijl. But one must note the differences: what fascinated Scarpa about this architectural language was not the deconstruction of space in imaginary surfaces but rather the possibility of discovering joints, such as the corner windows he sketched in such meticulous detail, in order to reconstitute the whole.

It is interesting to compare Scarpa's attitude towards the new spatial concept of Neoplasticism with the reactions exhibited by other architects who were of the same generation, but who operated in a different cultural ambience, for example one that was closer to that of Frank Lloyd Wright than to that of Ludwig Mies van der Rohe. In this context I think of Richard Neutra and Rudolph Schindler, who, with their Viennese

Italian Pavilion, 34th Biennale, Venice, 1968
Creation of the ellipsoidal pattern on the new entrance façade

Sketch for the renovation of the *Aula Magna*
of the Ca' Foscari in Venice, 1935

backgrounds and tendency to devote attention to detail, can be compared with Scarpa. Although both of them were students of Otto Wagner's, they nevertheless radically restructured his architecture; yet, all the while they never lost sight of his eye for detail and his feeling for the significance of materials. However, in drawing a comparison with Neutra and Schindler, I by no means wish to imply that Scarpa's architectural outlook resembled theirs, I only mean to say that he came upon the discovery of the new space by a similar path.

In the late 1960s, when Scarpa finally had the opportunity to become directly acquainted with the work of Frank Lloyd Wright, which had fascinated him for years and which he had long tried to imagine from publications, he was disappointed by its lack of individual structural elements which he considered the most decisive characteristic of the new architectural language. Scarpa's own formal language had attained self-sufficiency in these years, and architecture was in a state of radical change which alienated it from Wright's legacy ten years after his death. Louis Kahn was developing his "architecture of remembrance", which was closely related to Scarpa's design outlook in its attention to details and to joints. Kahn asserted that "the joint is the beginning of ornament".

When Scarpa applied the Neoplasticist decomposition of space, he considered not surfaces but instead their connections, the treatment of structural joints and hinges as well as the development of elements like corner windows. Instead of formulating a repertory of rectangular areas without stipulating their location (floor, wall, ceiling) and thus attaining the abstraction of the Dutch De Stijl, Scarpa stressed the joints and sought to enhance them by dissociating the whole into its component parts. With Scarpa this *dissoziation* (to use his term) was not an intentional breach of the rules, but instead was the only way he could introduce the joints that would allow the architecture to speak, without relapsing into the ornamentation on which the modern movement had turned its back.

Scarpa used these spatial "prepositions" in order to preserve the figurative character of classical architecture by means of formal figures that originated in what has become "nature" in the modern age. Instead of leaves and blossoms, his joints depict elements drawn from the most sophisticated technology, precision instruments, cameras, gauges, etc.

Scarpa knew how much the loss of ornament—showing, at the joints, what the compositional elements are doing—would silence architecture. Moulding, lesenes, cornices, angles, etc. show how the elements of a building attack and repel each other, or are somehow contorted, while their disappearance leaves all relations between these elements in limbo. Scarpa's designs were intended to supersede all these ancient architectural "prepositions".

Detail and Craftsmanship

Scarpa did not believe that the employment of architectural figures in keeping with the skills inherent in individual building trades (carpenters, marble carvers, cabinetmakers, or blacksmiths) should simply be limited to having craftsmen merely forming something, or executing a drawing, but rather meant engaging in creative reflection, which was a constant source of inspiration in his design of unusual details. Extensive discussions with craftsmen, which accompanied the development and final determination of many episodes in Scarpa's architecture, bear witness to the exchange of

Left page:
Renovation of the *Aula Magna* of the
Ca' Foscari, Venice, 1955–1956

Sculpture garden, Italian Pavilion, 26th Biennale, Venice, 1952

knowledge and to the constructive craft basis from which the syntax of his architectural language developed.

His draft design provided this constructive reflection of the craft with a script; it provided a score for the craftsmen's motifs. For Scarpa, draughtsmanship was comparable to the virtuosity of a performing musician: it demanded the same manual skill and was accompanied by an analogous visual control. The drawing followed its own tradition; it too had its own form of virtuosity, its own technique of instrumentation.

Scarpa's decomposition was therefore determined by the progress of the building work. The "cut" of the various elements was a product of the context of the work, even when it was carried out by different craftsmen. In his first attempts at the architecture of decomposition, under the influence of the Secession, his "fragments" can be taken as episodes of construction. In the first stage of his development he created a union between the workshop and the Academy, after a period of increasing estrangement that had followed the separation of design and construction. Hence, in my opinion, a technical interpretation of Scarpa's designs is more appropriate than the usual highly formal approach.

The influence of the Secession school came to be felt far more strongly in Venetian visual arts after the First World War. Having made first inroads in the wake of the Biennale, it encountered highly favourable conditions in Venice as a result of the strong tradition of local artisans. The many carpenters, stone masons, glaziers, plasterers, etc., whose skills were so highly valued by the local building trade, were given a great boost in prestige as a result of the decorative innovations of Secession architecture. Their feeling for materials, their ability to combine textures, as demonstrated by their cornices, the care they look in their joints, and their clever treatment of details, all indicate a consummate skill, which an architect like Scarpa would feel impelled to use.

Scarpa did not restrict himself to using the available skills, but cultivated communication with the people who were to implement his drawings, developing both their skills and their creativity. He thus revived an artisan culture which had been threatened with disappearance. He enhanced it by designs which made the culture relevant, integrating it with contemporary architecture. Moreover, he showed that one could restructure existing buildings by employing almost-forgotten techniques of working with wood, marble, iron and stucco which provided a link between the new and the old.

With his conviction that one can learn by doing, during the course of production, Carlo Scarpa also reintroduced the intellectual element into the culture of craftsmanship which had typified the drafting of designs since the early Renaissance. Following Giovanni Battista Vico's maxim, *verum ipsum factum*, Scarpa emphasized that one reaches the truth through manual constructional work, a thought akin to the logic of dialectical reasoning.

Visualisation

When, after finishing my studies, I joined Scarpa's team as an apprentice, I found his ability to continue to develop his thoughts while producing his drawings extraordinarily instructive. I was able to observe directly how his thoughts evolved on paper. His highly personal way of linking the various formal figures together followed a logic which was completely different from the normal conceptual logic that is derived from language. It seemed instead to be inspired by a figurative rationality that demanded steps to be taken that at first appeared to be unnecessary or all too obvious, but which then proved to be highly productive. Since then I have been fascinated by this figurative thinking and I am always attempting to understand its laws, its applications and its connection to architectural compostion.

This figurative thinking which takes place while the design is being sketched out thus also characterized the forms of referentiality, which are the point of departure for Scarpa's compositional language. They coincide with those of the system of Neoplasticism, which means that they explain primarily through examples, even when they retain the referential mode of depiction, of quotation and of expression in the details. Scarpa frequently warned his students and staff to distrust pictorial representation in architecture. He maintained that if what we were drawing resembled anything, then it should be erased.

Ticket kiosk to the garden, 26th Biennale, Venice, 1952

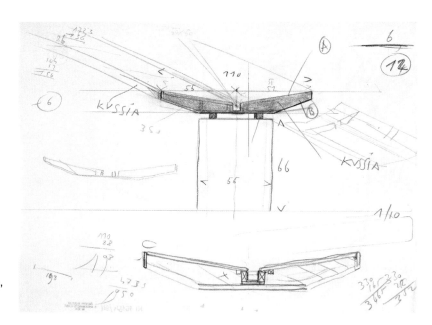

Palazzo Querini-Stampalia, Venice, 1961–1963, cross section of the visitors' bench
The drawing cites measurements and materials.

Like most modern architects, Scarpa was of the opinion that shapes have no denotative meanings. Architectural forms, he thought, refer purely to themselves, and are based on a non-denotative referentiality, they are auto-referential and exemplary.

That at least was the theory. But once its normative character had begun to wear off, Scarpa was free to develop to the full the referential complexity of his style. The knots and seams, which represented, along with facing and texture, the point of departure for architecture in Gottfried Semper's opinion, constitute the motifs which permit the static approach to representation to be overcome by pointing towards a programmatic and dynamic dimension. If dancing is the poetic mode of walking, then it is the skill of the carpenter, the stonemason or the weaver which gives form to architectural motifs, translating them into poetic modes of building. If one regards this dynamic, operational concept of figurative representation as a materialist approach to architectural theory, the logical consequence is the abolition of the referential symbolic dimension. When, in the 1960s, I wrote a lecture for my students in which I explained how with Scarpa, a design came about through the drawing process, I described this process as poetic. This aspect provides further motivation for the non-denotative character of Scarpa's compositional language. The language of poetry is centred on itself: it is "opaque" with respect to its content. On this point, the intuitive thoughts on the non-transparency of the visual arts are entirely correct, but only by virtue of their specifically poetic-artistic character, and not of their visual nature, as the psychology of visual perception would have it.

In poetic language, form is so important that it is difficult if not impossible to distinguish it from the content to which it refers. Seen thus, Scarpa's compositions seem to have no content other than their form. The exemplificatory referentiality and the poetic character of their communication conceal their textual dimension. Scarpa's hinges and joints between his double columns are examples of the clever technology of the scientific apparatus, the cut-outs in the panels and the zig-zag outlines are examples of the carpentry of classical architecture. They do not visually reproduce those

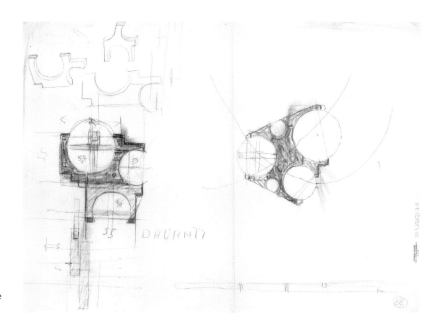

**Restoration of the Museum of Ancient Arms,
Castello di Brescia, Brescia, 1971**
Detail drawing of the supporting elements of the
balustrade

mechanical technologies found in some engineering transpositions, nor do they reflect the simple templates of the orders as in the historicist style. Scarpa's works exemplify the rhythms, the movements and the textures of the referents, in the sense that they share precisely these qualities with them and make their relevance clear. Scarpa's aim was a tighter and more articulated language of formal elements in order to reveal them as shapes.

There are studies that attempt to document a new, original form of referentiality in the abstract figures in Scarpa's architecture, such as the one by Francesco Dal Co on the occasion of the 1984 Venice exhibition. The conclusions of these studies have been confirmed by the many marginal notes in books offered for inspection by Scarpa's widow, Signora Nini. Scarpa had clearly made repeated use of these works. I agree with Francesco Dal Co's thesis that one can detect in Scarpa's formal elements references to archetypal symbols, which our civilization has forgotten but which are still active. The non-literal, metaphorical exemplification of these referents entails an Expressionist interpretation of these compositional elements. The alternation between exemplification and expression, the hallmark of Carlo Scarpa's symbolic system, would confirm its non-denotative referentiality and explain the poetic tension, two elements which breathe life into his architectural works. It would also explain his influence as a teacher, once certain Modernist prohibitions had lost their authority. The eminently practical nature of Functionalist forms explains the confusion between text and tool (the residential building as a "machine à habiter"), which resulted in Scarpa's so-called formalism being relegated to the realm of decoration.

In 1963, Carlo Scarpa was finally made a full professor, but the chair was that of Decorazione. Considering the status of "the ornamental" at that time, we can see what the academic establishment, his purported supporters, really thought of his explorations in architectural composition. The geometric decorative schemes did not represent anything visually and they also lacked the type of pseudo-referents that were akin to functions in the Modernist movement. Accordingly, for him, ornaments were only meant to exemplify, and this was also how Scarpa perceived many abstract paintings, particularly those generated as computer graphics or Op art. It is by no means a coincidence that Ernst Gombrich established a relationship between abstract art and the disappearance of decoration.

Experiment on the Work of Art

In Scarpa's architecture, light—to focus on an important aspect of his concept of space—became the "symbolic system" that allowed him to bring an institution like a museum and the works of art that constitute it into a discourse and to thereby understand them. At the Gipsoteca in Possagno, for example, Scarpa "put" the sculpture of Antonio Canova "in the proper light"; it is an especially diaphanous light, which has become an extraordinary instrument of architectural criticism, much more effective than the verbiage of the art critics.

I had seen the Canova statues once before, in the 1950s, before they were moved to Scarpa's annex. To see them here came as a revelation. Scarpa had made room for the sculptures by putting them in just the right light. They are, what constitutes the space in which they stand, so that it would be unthinkable to rearrange or remove them. This act of establishing space in the light, that means bringing them into the light—creating space in contrast to the abstract space of technical modernity—not only shows the works, it also reveals their meaning. This architecture makes comprehensible that thesis of the philosophy of art which maintains that in the existence of a work of art, the labours of those who produce and those who conserve coincide. It is the work itself which brings its creator into being and requires the existence of those who conserve it. Hence, by this interpretation, the sculptures in the Gipsoteca become works of art through both Canova's and Scarpa's efforts.

I should therefore like to consider architecture as the art of light, and the luminous space created by Carlo Scarpa as the cognitive instrument employed to make things clear. Scarpa's explorations were concerned more with Canova's sculptures than with the building which was to house them as if it were a question of writing/building an architectural essay on the sculptures. Even if "discourse" (i.e. the mode in which the essay/the Gipsoteca is organized) is just as important as the "history" that they tell in Scarpa's text, it seems important to me to clarify the difference that is determined by whether this architecture is queried as a text or as a tool. As a text, the Gipsoteca can express a content, exemplify a type and its characteristics; as a tool, as an "exhibition machine", it can only function, at best entertain the visitors with its quiet charm.

The work which Scarpa expended on the Canova statues was architecture used as a form of criticism, but in my opinion a criticism closely akin to the Romantic concept, which viewed criticism as the consummation of a work of art, rather than as a judgement passed on it. For Carlo Scarpa, criticism was an experiment on the work of art, awakening the reflection by which the work becomes aware of itself. Scarpa's architecture functions as a system of symbols, as an architectural language, which, being a language, becomes a "means" for the recognition/production of reality rather than the "object" of such a recognition/production. It seems important to me to bring out this reversal of architectural design vis-à-vis Functionalist ideology, according to which—by contrast—the work is what is set up by the search as the goal of understanding.

The hermeneutic approach of Scarpa's architecture explains its critical power and is the key to understanding his zeal to use architecture for the display of works of art,

Vase with coloured horizontal stripes, Venini & C., Murano, 1940

a zeal which characterizes much of his output. In this regard, Scarpa's compositional search anticipates the "weak project" that now enlivens architectural discussions.

Many of the difficulties experienced by critics in accepting Scarpa's work as genuine architecture were due to his tendency to design in fragments, to the way in which his projects grew around a pre-existing nucleus, and to his continual revision of what was already on the drawing board. It would be interesting to study the connection between Minimal Art and Conceptualism, which is oriented on the scientific fundamentals of logical positivism. The concept of art characterized by contemporary analytical philosophy—here one thinks above all of Nelson Goodman—emerged from the encounter between European logical positivism and American pragmatism. It provides a very viable critical instrument for gaining an understanding of Scarpa's architecture.

Within the larger context of the ongoing dissipation of the foundation, which determined the crisis of academic design methods like the architecture of rationalism, Scarpa's work was aimed at local complexities which were becoming increasingly autonomous and independent of any centre or hierarchy. Scarpa did not respond to this loss of a centre with any analytical approach, resolving the whole into ready-made self-sufficient units; rather, he put forward a programme which proceeded piece by piece, the fragmentary nature of which kept open the hermeneutic circularity which is characteristic of the interpretation of texts as well as being the hallmark of Carlo Scarpa's architecture.

To this insight that things belong together, an insight which brings to a focus the relational character of Scarpa's details, can be added another aspect of the relationship between the whole and its parts, namely an awareness of the dialogue in which the design came about. Scarpa's work always implies an interplay between those who speak the same language, who share a particular system of symbols. The design process, if understood as interpretive, is based on the understanding that the project belongs to a particular context using a particular architectural language. This description of Carlo Scarpa's approach to design leads us to the question of restoration and history.

Gavina Showroom, Bologna, 1961–1963
Detail of the access to the cash desk

Design and Context

When Scarpa worked on new projects in historical contexts, this preference of his for building on existing structures was much deprecated, and even Bruno Zevi, who was always very supportive of the results, felt compelled to describe him as "a great artist, but not an architect". Today, this interest is looked upon as Scarpa's greatest virtue. Opposing contemporary trends in architecture, he refused to heed the siren voices of utopianism, and explored regions remote from the missionary zeal of the ideologists. Since Scarpa, it has come to be recognized that many of the designs of the great architects of the past were likewise developed in historical contexts: Brunelleschi, Alberti, Bramante, Palladio and Borromini all built, like Scarpa, on existing structures.

Scarpa's preference for designing new things in a historical context should be seen alongside his other favourite activity, museum design. The link between these two predilections was his ability to "read", to decipher "pictorial texts", in the form of an existing building or in the pictures and sculptures which were to be displayed. It is this peculiar faculty, this figurative competence, which characterizes Scarpa's creative process. Thus we have drawn together three threads which seem to me fundamental to an understanding of his architecture: his design process, based on this visual competence (i.e. the drawing), his interest in museum design, and his creative restoration of existing

buildings. In all these instances, Scarpa seemed to develop an architectural dialogue with the existing shapes. His museums are never merely neutral spaces into which just any works of art could be placed; rather, they represent critical and conscious decisions, which, taking the exhibits as their starting point, complement them in a way essential to their understanding, they are—as a new museology suggests—installations.

This approach to architectural composition, which I have compared to the figurative approach of the Renaissance architect and painter, also helps explain the relation between project and history. Scarpa employed a figurative language whose effectiveness was backed up by an intrinsic historicity. His attitude to history has nothing in common with the sort of academic historicism which uses a study of the architecture of the past to exploit its themes, shapes and lay-outs as though it were a warehouse of "ready-made phrases", to use an expression of Adolf Loos'. For Carlo Scarpa, history was a codex consolidated by tradition, breathing meaning into the shapes conjured up on the design by drawing. One can discern in his architectural approach this common language, this familiar vocabulary, which links the different visual arts across the whole design. If a project continues after the death of its architect, it must be finished by

Museo di Castelvecchio, Verona, 1956–1964

someone who, knowing this language, can bring it to completion. This handing-down of a project from generation to generation, which was already common enough, is now becoming the norm where "civic architecture" is concerned. Squares and streets are "rooms", whose interior walls are the façades of houses dating from different epochs. Continuity becomes quite precarious when there is no shared language. Scarpa's figurative system in architecture is thus an original contribution towards overcoming the many difficulties encountered by contemporary designs when they involve intervention in a historical context.

Light and Space

Having adopted a system of architecture akin to that of the Secession, Scarpa wanted to turn the act of construction into a process of communication and understanding. This "understanding" aspect of the artistic process has been explained by Conrad Fiedler in an essay devoted to architecture, in which he based his own reflections on the theories of Gottfried Semper. In order to reach a better understanding of this aspect of design, we should look at the transition of Scarpa's compositional system in comparison to that of the Secession, by reference to one decisive element of composition in modern architecture, namely the window.

It is no coincidence that windows play an important role in the interpretation of architecture from the point of view of the immediate surroundings and regional context. A study of the window makes it possible to trace the development of an opening in the frontage intended as an "aedicule", "loggia" or "porch", into a "bay window". A further development, leading Scarpa to a new concept of space, made possible the step from "bay windows" to "corner windows". This second step, even more decisive than the first, was the transition from Secession to Neoplasticism, embodied in the work of Frank Lloyd Wright.

Neutra and Schindler, like Scarpa, took up this discovery, while preserving their feeling for solid craftsmanship. I do not, of course, mean to compare Scarpa's architecture to that of Schindler and Neutra, but it is interesting to recognize this new concept of space, which had influenced Mies van der Rohe and before him the Dutchmen who developed the architecture of De Stijl.

The new concept was described most succinctly by Wright as "The Destruction of the Box". Scarpa adopted it, eliminating the traditional corners of rooms, but provided the dissociated surfaces with highly articulated joints. It has been pointed out, and rightly, that De Stijl represents the most systematic codification of modern architectural language; if one accepts curved surfaces and non-orthogonal lay-outs, Neoplasticism, along with Le Corbusier's "5-point system" is the most widespread version of modern architectural "grammar".

I shall address the paradigm of the room functioning as an "inverted chandelier", and consider more closely how the change came about from rooms in the classical style to those built under the Secession, in order to describe the transition to De Stijl. To understand the relevance of these observations we must bear in mind the chief variables in an illuminated space, light sources and light diffusers. Fenestrated rooms that function as "inverted chandeliers" involve particular combinations of light sources and light diffusers. On the one hand, we have the almost completely glazed rooms of Gothic architecture; on the other, we have Classical architecture with its regular apertures, niches and porches. In the northern countries, rooms have bay windows to catch

Museo di Castelvecchio, Verona, 1956–1964
Design and installation of an ivory sculpture of
Maria with the Christ Child

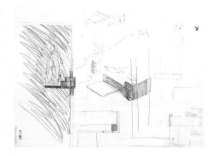

as much light as possible, while rooms in Mediterranean lands have to be protected from the sunlight by shades and blinds. Even a porch is a means of filtering out excessive light and preventing glare.

Corner windows, an invention of the Modernist movement, produce a room in which the glazed apertures—the light sources—and the walls—the surfaces that diffuse this light—are at right angles to each other. This solution avoids the dazzle resulting from a window in the middle of the wall, where the only diffusers are well away from the light source. Once it is realized that light can be modulated by an opportune combination of sources and diffusers, a new level of architectural quality becomes possible.

Scarpa was familiar with similar windows installed close to the side wall in order to distribute the sunlight from Venetian palazzi. He used coloured surfaces, white walls, water, etc. as diffusers in his buildings, combining them with various sources of direct, indirect or artificial light. With light sources and diffusing surfaces at right angles to each other, as with corner windows, the walls become illumination systems that colour the light through their own material textures. Thus the techniques with which Scarpa created the effect of a diffused brightness, which is characteristic of the space he created in the museum in Possagno, can be both understood and replicated.

And almost as if he wanted to give the work a certain intimacy, by forcing the two levels that essentially constitute the building together and extricate it, he simply moves a horizontal element up alongside the Gipsoteca, in order to protect the plaster cases from sun and rain, as well as a vertical element in order to screen out the urban context. At the spot where the water generates a dappled, animated light as a result of the effects caused by the wind on its surface, Scarpa placed the Three Graces. This subdued light interprets, better than any commentary, the mythological femininity of the dancing girls. This then changes radically when crossing over to the corner window, to the space that is actually illuminated. The light characterizes this change, which defines the new space. In order to pursue the first transition of the architectural language, one must consider the introduction of a "bay window", so highly prized by the Secession—and especially by Hoffmann—into this classical space. This brings us to Wagner and also to Sullivan. Subsequently Wright created his Prairie houses, which might be seen as the arrangement of a series of "bay windows" accompanied by the ongoing elimination of the spaces that belong to them. He was subsequently able to transform the "bay windows" into three-dimensional hinges between levels—which were dis-associated in order to prevent "the box" from being reconstituted—and he thereby created the sort of combination of light sources and light dispersers at the corners that establish a new space: space perceived as depth, not just in its circumference. Scarpa's compositional system, as displayed in the treatment of windows and light, makes use of two developments characteristic of modern architecture. The first one made the "bay window" of the Secession out of the classical aedicule, and in the second one it then became the corner window as found in the works of Wright or De Stijl.

Furthermore, one compositional technique introduced by Scarpa may, I think, be derived from the architecture of the towns in the Veneto. For this purpose, it is suffi-cient to recall Scarpa's projects of the 1950s, with their corner windows. Apart from the Possagno gallery, these include the Casa Veritti in Udine, and some unfinished projects such as the Villa Zoppas in Conegliano and the Casa Taddei in Venice. He translated the corner windows of the new spatial concept into the vocabulary of the Veneto: the light produced by these corner windows becomes a chromatic luminosity full of trans-parency, typical of the region's visual arts for centuries.

In the Venezuelan Pavilion on the Venice Biennale site, Scarpa covered the corner windows of the two halls with latticed shades, reminiscent of similar solutions to the problem of filtering the light. His rooms have a luminosity, which, apart from the manifestly different vocabulary, generate the flowing light of Palladio and his seven-teenth and eighteenth century successors. Along the way, Scarpa's Venetian language was enriched by other important design elements when he moved from shaded corner windows to the double façade claddings borrowed by Louis Kahn and Robert Venturi from the Baroque.

For the Banca Popolare di Verona he designed windows that are more or less the reverse of bay windows. He based them on a type he had seen many years before in an ugly building in Genoa across the street from the Hotel Bristol where he was staying in conjunction with plans for a new building for the Teatro di Genua. The new window openings in the double casing projected outwards and were of a different shape; they took up less space than the opening on the inside, in which the casements were in-stalled. Scarpa realized that the light reflected by the glass would be diffused by the inner surface of the outer cladding, thus reducing the glare and improving the lighting within. This solution, even nearer to Palladio and the Veneto, using layered, transpar-ent surfaces, allowed windows to be placed centrally in a wall while avoiding the con-comitant effect of tiresome glare. Such a room, whose character is conditioned by its double fenestration—a central aspect of my own architectural explorations—most effectively achieves the typical light of the Veneto countryside and its paintings, a light which is central to the identity and culture of the region and its landscape.

This capacity of architecture to take root in places, and thereby bring out the genius loci and make it speak, is growing even more important with the increase in inter-national exchanges. In this connection, the role of light is of paramount importance. While a design worked out in the international style—even in its postmodern manifest-ation—can be envisaged in isolation from its physical site, a design which takes ac-count of the effect of architecture on its environment has no choice but to put down roots there.

Banca Popolare di Verona, 1973–1982
Main façade overlooking the Piazza Nogara

Gipsoteca Canoviana, Possagno, 1955–1957
Corner window in the new wing

The Drawing Process

Scarpa began a design by using one of the configurations which constantly recur in his work, and which acquire a particular significance when inserted into a plan or elevation in order to fulfil syntactically defined functions in the building in question. The drawings reveal different attempts to combine these configurations, along with gradual changes in metric proportions which Scarpa referred to as "filing down". All these operations in the design process were structured in a specific manner, while the actual medium was changed: tracing paper, cardboard, drawing board, scale model, etc.

The drawing on cardboard fixed to the drawing board embraced the total complex—the whole building, for example—and developed slowly and cumulatively as the solutions worked out for various problems were filled in. This drawing board version was the frame of reference for the whole project from start to finish.

From this comprehensive drawing, the individual problems were extracted to be tackled on a different scale; these constituted the chief formal events of the design process. These drawings, which were developed on an "elephant scale" on ochre-coloured card, allowed a more in-depth study of the problem concerned, and were the

House Zentner, Zurich, 1964–1968
Frontal view and cross section of the fixtures
at the window for the curtains

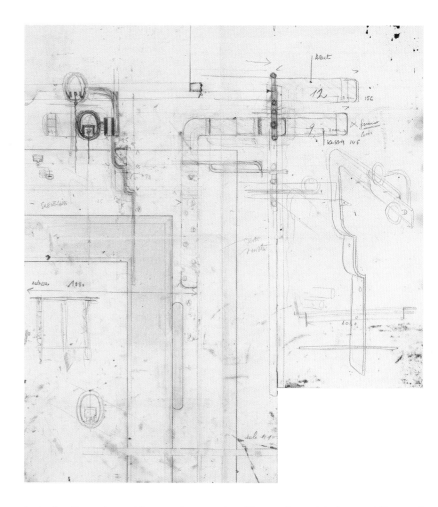

basis for discussions with consultants and staff, as well as with the specialists and craftsmen who were to do the calculations or construct the individual elements, as the case might be.

Drafting a problem on card produced a certain organizational structure that followed the reference points of the project: the axes, any specifications available, the dimensions, context-determined constraints, etc. Using overlays of tracing paper, it was possible to try out variations on the theme drawn on the card. These variations contained proposals which could be inserted into the base drawing to become, in their turn, modified by set procedures. When a variant on tracing paper was considered satisfactory, it was transferred to the drawing board and inserted into the completed parts of the total design. A problem thus abstracted from the whole necessitated the treatment of other problems, which were then tackled along the same lines.

In Scarpa's composition work, the card drawing on the drawing board formalized the allocation of the selected configurations; the ochre-card drawing defined the dissection of the work into specific formal events, and thus the syntactic organization of the system, while the tracing-paper put into effect the transformations characteristic of Scarpa's design procedure. The sequence of continuous gradual change—seen on comparing the many tracing-paper versions—shows clearly how the composition evolved;

moreover, they have an argumentative character, transforming them into true figurative inferences.

This way of splitting the design process into formal events resulting from the construction operations could give the false impression with regard to the context. While these episodes do indeed appear as fragments, they are like this so as to evoke the totality from which they proceed. As in much recent architecture, Scarpa's shapes are manifested in simple signs, details and fragments—never as complete units. And yet they point to complexes to which they are virtually linked, so that one senses interpenetrations, overlaps and intertwinings that hint at an underlying hierarchical structure. In Scarpa's architecture it is difficult to find the juxtaposition of clearly defined volumes typical of the design procedure of the Neoclassicists in which elements were arranged one alongside the other.

In connection with rules of proportion and scale which accompanied and controlled the "filing down", mention should be made of Scarpa's interest in the geometrical conundrums of Matila Ghyka. One can see how in his last projects, such as the Banca Popolare di Verona, when he was moving towards what might be called a regionalist grammar, he was reverting to a Classical architectural system, although this had more to do with the hierarchic mode employed in Baroque or Mannerist architecture than with the character of Neoclassicism where elements are arranged alongside each other. If we recognize the Veneto ingredient in Scarpa's architecture, we should refer to the special qualities of Venetian classicism, which, unlike that of Alberti, Bramante or Brunelleschi, never relied on composition with three-dimensional cells. Rather, he goes back to Serlio, Sanmicheli, Sansovino, Palladio, Scamozzi, etc., with their transparent shapes and stratifications which seem to better explain much of the complexity of Carlo Scarpa's architecture.

1952–1953, 1957–1960 ▸ Museo Correr

Historical Collection and Quadreria ▸ Piazza San Marco, Venice

Opposite page:
The Bellini Hall, 1957–1960

Right:
Exhibition hall for showcases and sculpture, 1957–1960

Below:
Plinth for the statue of the Doge Antonio Venier by Jacobello delle Masegne, 1957–1960

For the Museo Correr, Carlo Scarpa redesigned the exhibition of historical artefacts and paintings. This took place over a period of eight years with intermittent interruptions and had to come to terms with architecture which had his own strong character. The Museum of Venetian Art and History is in the Procuratie Nuove on the Piazza San Marco. If one enters via the monumental stairway of the Ala Napoleonica, one first encounters the historical and ethnographic collection on the first floor, and then the painting collection on the second floor. Scarpa's work began with redesigning of the historical department, whereby the diversity of the objects on exhibition—including coins, garments, weapons, flags, documents and the work of goldsmiths—represented a particular challenge. Later he concentrated on re-ordering the painting collection, which meant exhibiting a cohesive complex of artwork in an enormous room. Scarpa's mastery as an exhibition architect is reflected in his ability to present all of these objects in a manner suited to the specific character of each of the individual pieces.

Scarpa adopted the structure of the floor plan, which ran parallel to the Piazza San Marco, by presenting the paintings on wooden easels at right angles to the windows. This allowed him to emphasize the symmetry of the longitudinal axes along both sides of the Procuratie.

1952–1972 · Exhibition Design

Exhibition "The Sense of Colour and the Rule of the Waters", Turin, 1961

Apart from museum architecture, exhibition design—temporary architecture—was a central element in Scarpa's work. His exhibition designs could be seen in Milan, Turin, Florence, Rome, London, Paris, Montreal, San Francisco and—above all—time and again in Venice. In 1972, with his show "Aspects of Modern Italian Sculpture", he ended thirty years of cooperation with the Venice Biennale. The main intention of his exhibition work was to take over the "language" of the works on display and to "speak" the same way in his design. He aimed at an amplification which in no small way enhanced an understanding of the exhibits. His ability to exhibit art in a charismatic, fascinating way thus comes as no surprise. What art critics say in words, Scarpa said in space, surface, colour and light. The interrelations he created between the exhibits and architecture were true "labels" of his achievement.

Just as he could not design a building without knowing where it was to be built, he could not design an exhibition room without knowing what was to be displayed. The two aspects are connected by the idea of always concentrating on dialogue, avoiding the expression of one's personal intuitions in isolation.

Italian Pavilion, 34th Biennale, Venice, 1968
Inauguration of the new façade

Italian Pavilion, 36th Biennale, Venice, 1972
Hall of the sculptor Valeriano Trebbiani in the
section *Aspects of Contemporary Italian
Sculpture*

Carlo Scarpa never simply hung a ready-framed picture on the wall; he always designed a three-dimensional context for the work on exhibition.

Light is always fundamental: often it is adjusted with great sensitivity; sometimes it is brutal, achieving effects which do not simply display something but prescribe a certain path, certain interruptions or vetoes for the eye. Light and colour are not neutral; they comment, explain, interpret and describe. Scarpa's exhibitions were never boring.

1953–1954 ▸ Galleria Regionale di Sicilia

Renovation of the Palazzo Abatellis as a Museum ▸ Palermo
▸ with Roberto Calandra

Opposite page:
Colonnaded hall with a stairway, the stairs of which have a hexagonal cross section

Right:
Halls of Gagini and Laurana

Rotating support for a woman's head by Francesco Laurana

Scarpa received this commission after designing an exhibition of the works of Antonello da Messina in Messina in 1953. The gallery needed to be rennovated quickly, and this forced Scarpa to work on site rather than in his usual meditative manner. The Palazzo Abatellis was built by Matteo Carnilivari between 1490 and 1526. Scarpa's renovation wove the artworks and the building together so skilfully that both were shown to their best advantage.

The building is laid out on a rectangular plan with its arcade oriented towards the inner courtyard which is paved with river gravel, a feature the architect retained. On the façade, Scarpa set the window frames slightly off to the side behind the triple-arched openings with arabesque motifs in order not to diminish their beauty. He transferred a building technique in which various levels are laid one over the other from Venice to Palermo.

His instinctive sensibility in dealing with works of art and his cultivated sense for the figurative allowed him to choose the illumination, materials and colours in an adept manner. In this sense, he also suggested a tour round the museum that encouraged visitors to pause in front of important objects, piquing their curiosity and allowing them to view works again and again from different perspectives, while circling a sculpture, or by turning a painting in such a way that it could be viewed in a better light.

1955–1957 ▸ Gipsoteca Canoviana
New Wing ▸ Piazza Canova, Possagno, Treviso ▸ with Valeriano Pastor

Corner window in the new wing built by Carlo Scarpa

In 1955, to commemorate the two hundredth anniversary of the birth of Antonio Canova, Carlo Scarpa was asked by the Soprintendenza alle Belle Arti to extend the Canova Museum at Possagno, so as to rehouse the artist's copies, original plaster casts, marble sculptures and terracotta designs, which till then had been too tightly crammed together. The Venetian architect Francesco Lazzari had been commissioned by Monsignor Sartori to build the existing Gipsoteca, which is laid out on a basilica plan, in 1832 and it was opened upon its completion in 1836. It was therefore one of the first structures to be designed specifically as a museum.

The elongated site available to Scarpa, in a road sloping down the valley, was not large. Scarpa built the roof to resemble a waterfall that originates at the top of the hall running down between two converging walls and ending with a glass wall facing a pool of water. He thus multiplied the possible views and placed the sculptures in such a way as to strengthen the contrast between the abstract white of the plaster and the vital realism of the recumbent or upright female bodies. In this connection Carlo Scarpa spoke of a frame effect. At the far end of the long extension, where the water surface ruffled by the wind reflects a shimmering light, Scarpa placed the group of the *Three Graces*. This hesitant brilliance, so to speak, interprets well the mythical femininity of the dancing girls.

To achieve a well-modulated, varied light in the room, Scarpa consciously arranged for openings where the walls joined, creating corner windows. The light is thus always thrown onto a vertical diffusing surface, appreciably reducing the glare of normal windows. But there was another curious result: "I wanted to cut up the blue of the sky," commented Scarpa.

Of the two long walls which form the new extension, the solid windowless outer wall on the side towards the road reflects the light back into the display area, providing an appropriate background for the contours of the sculptures. The second wall, parallel to the existing museum, allows for a narrow path between the old and the new building. Its front part is a steel frame filled with glass or soft Vicenza stone with "peephole" windows.

Each statue is specially placed for the space and the light it needs, which may be glaring or else gently caresses the plaster-casts, giving them various appearances with the changes of the day, the season or the weather. Giuseppe Mazzariol therefore speaks of "actors in stone"; the visitor has the impression of sharing the lives of these sculptures.

For the wall plaster, Scarpa said his first spontaneous idea was for a dark background for the pale sculptures. But pondering the effect of this contrast on the adjacent hall where the statues stand against grey walls, Scarpa decided to keep the unexpected play of white against white we now take so much for granted. A dark background would not have shown the three-dimensionality of the sculptures as clearly, but would have instead more strongly emphasized the two-dimensional silhouette. The interior walls are painted pale white and the exterior walls are plastered with *graniglia*.

Opposite page:
Large hall with three-part windows
In the foreground the showcases with terracotta models, behind the plaster model for *The Sleeping Nymph*

In the foreground the plaster model for *The Sleeping Nymph*, to the right the plaster sculpture of a seated George Washington

The Sleeping Nymph, a bust of Napoleon and, in the showcase, the terracotta portrait of the Princess Leopoldina Esterházy

The wing that leads to the glass wall facing south, in the foreground a plaster model for *Dirce* as a reclining nude

The display cases are mounted on simple iron stands, with the glass held together by brass hardware. The large glass enclosure for the Three Graces posed a particular problem at that time, because large sheets of glass were not yet available. Scarpa therefore had the panes of glass cut in different places; in order to prevent the edges from becoming green or casting reflections, he left them unpolished and opaque.

Above:

From left to right: *George Washington Attired as a Roman General* (statue created for the State Capitol in Raleigh, North Carolina), a bust of Canova, a plaster model for a *Reclining Naiad*, a bozzetto of the Tomb of *Pope Clemens XIV, Amour and Psyche with the Butterfly*, another plaster model of a *Reclining Naiad*

Below:

Details in cross section and elevation of a door and window with measurements and materials

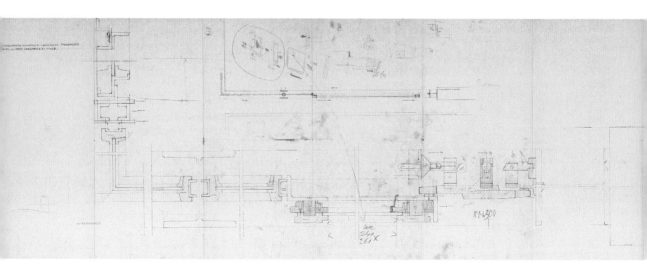

View from the south of the wing built by Scarpa, in the foreground the corner window overlooking the pond
The sunlight reflected in the water creates an ever-changing play of light on the *Three Graces Dancing*.

Southern side of the new wing

1955–1961 ▸ Casa Veritti

Viale Duodo, Udine ▸ with Carlo Maschietto, Federico Marconi, Angelo Morelli

View of the house from the southeast with the entrance in the east

Opposite page:
View of the dining room on the northwest side of the house

Carlo Scarpa received this commission from the lawyer Luigi Veritti, a relation of Angelo Masieri's, who shared Scarpa's interest in the architecture of Frank Lloyd Wright. The building site recommended by Scarpa was in a relatively undeveloped area, but the client decided on a long, narrow site on the edge of Udine. The project involved two main problems: first the long, narrow site and second the characterless district, neither town nor country, with residential buildings and workshops typical of the outskirts of a modern town.

On restricted sites, Scarpa liked curved structures. "One can have narrow passages as long as they widen at the end, and that is achieved with curved walls," he said. To avoid having a plan with right angles conditioned by the shape of the site, Scarpa drew a plan with two circles. But as the design developed, the second circle declined in importance and became a conservatory; the client wanted a more compact house which

View into the kitchen

The stairway leads to the upper storey where the bedrooms are located.

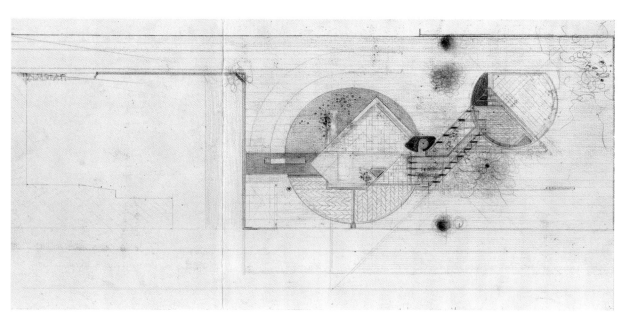

Design sketch of a previous solution, never realized

would therefore have to be on two storeys. But this attempt to harmonize the ideas of the architect with the wishes of the client also came to nothing.

Thus the house took on its present appearance: a protected space enclosed towards the north by a semi-circular wall, reminiscent of a snail shell, in order to shield it from the tramontana winds and the unwelcome inspection of passers-by, while to the south it is completely open in order to make the most of the sun and provide a view of less densely built up landscape. The circular figure, which is opened up by the glassed-in corridor with its many surfaces, is augmented by the contour of the pools of water in which the projecting façade is reflected, while the conservatory seems to grow out of the wall like a crystal. In Scarpa's architecture the column—alone or in series—was always a justification for creating sculpted elements. These often contributed to the rhythm of the space as a pivotal point in the composition, thereby both enhancing and concealing the structural function of the column. In this project, the rhythm of the large, hollow pilaster enriches the space with a number of new functions and meanings. From the garden gate, one reaches a small path, which leads to the boardwalk over the water basin and up to the entrance to the ground floor. The main axis of the site is oriented from east to west. When the house is approached from the east, the path leads along the southern edge of the property, so that the building initially presents itself from the southeast. This view is often seen in photographs. The space on the ground floor is only divided by built-in furniture made of mahogany and firwood, which were all designed by the architect.

1956–1964 ▸ Museo di Castelvecchio

Corso Castelvecchio, Verona ▸ with Carlo Maschietto, Arrigo Rudi

The entrance to the museum

In connection with the 1957 exhibition "Da Altichiero a Pisanello", Scarpa was commissioned only to restore the living quarters of the former citadel of Verona. But he did not limit himself to repairs; he tried by individual exposures and a little judicious demolition to reveal the different historical strata of the structural complex. He wanted to disentangle the periods of building, to address the building itself as a great archaeological find and to reveal the phases of enlargement and structural alteration through appropriate restorative intervention. Scarpa was more interested in historical transparency than in the theory of restoration; he wanted to make history come alive by a well-ordered juxtaposition of the fragments.

"Castelvecchio was all deception," said Carlo Scarpa in 1978, with regard to the elevation which leads to the courtyard. "I decided to introduce some vertical elements to break up the symmetry as the Gothic demanded; Gothic, especially in its Venetian form, is not very symmetrical." However, various hypothesis lead to the façade's ultimately appearing to be intact, although its "unnatural symmetry" has been "broken up" by adopting various interventions. The entrance first had to be moved away from the centre. Scarpa wanted the façade to stand out as a backcloth, and this he achieved

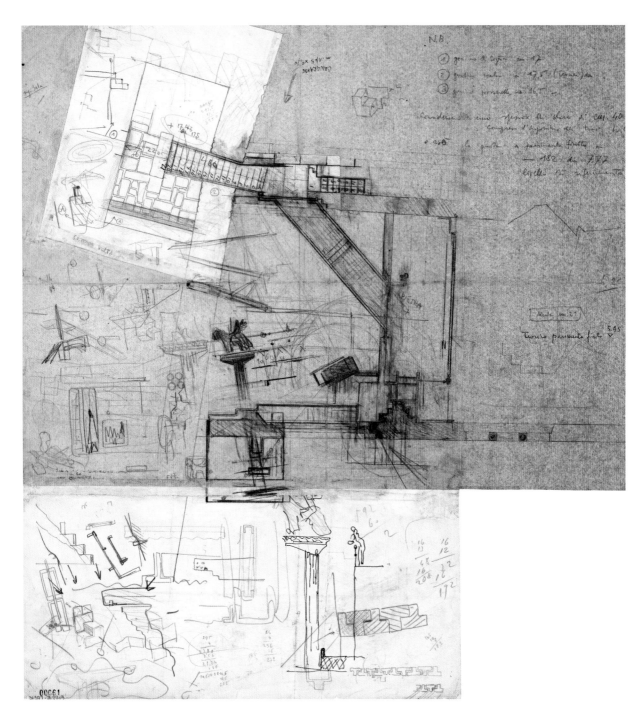

mainly by the fenestration. The windows are not related to the façade but to the internal walls.

Projecting elements such as the wall at the entrance or the floor areas were extended from inside to outside to help put across this inner wall as a part of the courtyard. Castelvecchio shows more than anywhere else how Scarpa's architecture is based on juxtaposition. There is a dialogue between different materials from different historical eras, placed close together yet apart. Hence the breaks: the newly-laid floors, like carpets, stop some distance short of the walls, while the walls in turn stop short of the ceilings.

Scarpa completely demolished a narrow strip of façade so as to expose the different hidden layers of the building. He made this break a place of synthesis for the whole structure and emphasized it by the statue of Cangrande della Scala. The statue stands where the historical interconnections are clearest, high up on a stone slab set askew on a concrete base. Near the entrance, almost hidden by a concrete crosswall, a small shrine stands out from the façade, a little chapel displaying precious Lombard "finds". Outside it is clad with small Prun stone slabs of different colour intensity, and alternately rough and smooth. Inside it is painted with bottle-green lime wash; the brick floor is edged with metal frames.

The exhibition rooms date from Napoleonic times and are arranged in sequence. Scarpa used subdued materials alternating with selected episodes as a commentary to frame the exhibits. The plaster is based on slaked lime, more or less rough, depending on the coarseness of the sand added. The concrete floors, which are divided into different fields, are edged with stone from Prun. The walls in the arched passages were clad with large rough slabs of pink Prun stone, familiar in the boundary walls of the old estates. An arched doorway with a grating of steel opens onto the great courtyard where the Cangrande statue stands.

A maze of steps at various levels, after Piranesi, made of rough-hewn concrete with narrow iron frames, leads to the western part of the courtyard inside the city walls. This leads to the Torre del Mastio and then on to the area displaying works by Veronese and

Design drawing of the façade of the Castelvecchio
Scarpa drew his proposals on a blueprint with coloured pencil.

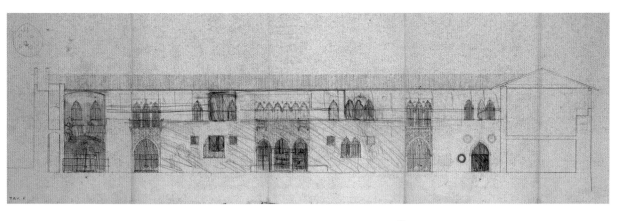

Venetian painters as well as some sculptures from the early Middle Ages up till the fifteenth century. It is possible to walk along the battlements so as to end one's tour in the gallery containing paintings from the fifteenth to the eighteenth centuries.

Some of Scarpa's tricks in the art displays are worth mentioning. Every exhibit had its own specially designed plinth, suspension or support. In the process he designed complete rooms with unusual combinations, using perspective to produce discoveries, aiming especially for the right light on each picture which fell from the side through the northern and southern windows.

He placed some pictures on the type of easel which he designed for the Museo Correr so as to allow the visitor to get very close to the picture. Elsewhere a picture may

Opposite page:
The sculpture gallery on the ground floor with works from the 12th to the 15th century

Below:
The fifth and last hall in the sculpture gallery
A "window" set into the floor affords a view of the recently excavated remains of an old moat.

The new stairway in the Reggia

Left:
Mounting of the exhibition of paintings in the Reggia, the residential wing of the old fortress

Right:
Upper Hall of Paintings

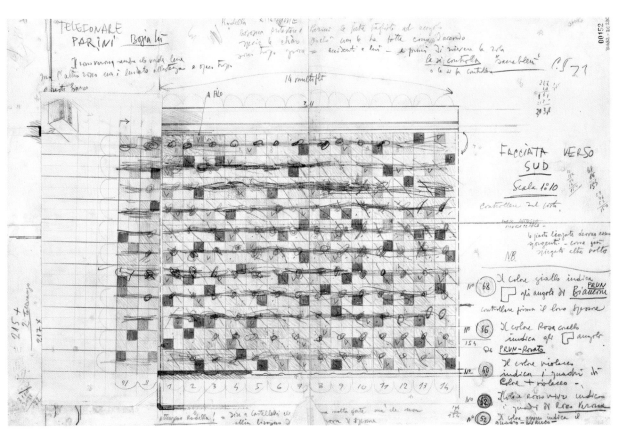

Wall development with instructions for the stoneworker

only gradually become visible or certain elements may be in a special way emphasized by the lighting.

For Scarpa museum architecture is not simply a way of housing art works, nor is it a display machine: it is a critical tool that makes art accessible and understandable.

1957–1958 ▸ Olivetti Showroom

Piazza San Marco, Venice ▸ with Gilda D'Agaro, Carlo Maschietto

Opposite page:
Display window and main entrance facing the marketplace

Right:
Side entrance

Scarpa was commissioned to design the Olivetti showroom on the Piazza San Marco in Venice after he and Ludovico Quaroni were awarded the Olivetti Prize for Architecture in 1956. Adriano Olivetti was without doubt a most important personality for Italian culture, one of the last great patrons. It is no surprise, therefore, that he entrusted the refurbishing to Carlo Scarpa, who at the time in question was little known in Italy.

The task was difficult: to exploit a narrow, long and relatively dark space that first had to be put into some sort of order. This meant strengthening the structure and removing the old fittings in order to carry out the real architectural surgery, which transformed the space by means of a gradual modulation of the light, from the display windows in the arcade to the rear window overlooking the canal with its delicate lattice of costly teak and rosewood filtering the reflections from the water. From every point, the room is seen as a whole. The upper level, reached by magnificent marble stairs, consists of long, low galleries lit by almond-shaped windows looking like eyes down onto the Piazza.

The passage through the room is eventful yet clearly outlined. Even the entrance from the side heralds the lack of symmetry in the inner passage. The little entrance hall is dominated by Alberto Viani's sculpture, which is reflected in a shallow black marble

View of the mezzanine level with the lenticular
windows overlooking the Piazza San Marco

pool. Further back is the staircase with its riserless stone steps hovering like a Neo-plastic deconstruction of Michelangelo's Laurenziana ramp, relaxing the stiff rect-angular space by its cascade of steps. This staircase of Aurisina marble leads up to the mezzanine level, whose parapet both links the spatial elements and sets them off against each other. The gallery side is panelled with African teak; the lower side over-looking the floor below has a polished Venetian hard-plaster surface.

Massive pilasters are a frequent motif in Scarpa's work. Stone slabs, ending unmis-takably below the level of the ceiling, advertise both their function as mere cladding and the montage quality of the ensemble. The artificial light throughout comes from vertical strips of satin glass hiding fluorescent tubes. Individual lighting is provided by small ebony lamps on stainless steel standards.

The rhythmically placed display windows in the arcade are flush with the façade, without ledge, overhang or other shadowing. The thick glass is held in a brass frame. All connecting elements are sealed while the edges are bevelled at 45 degrees in order to soften the harshness of the rectangular frame. Scarpa designed elegant, miniature wooden trays hung from the ceiling so that the products might be displayed without

obstructing the lighting or the view into the room. The floor, 31 centimetres above the Piazza, is remarkable enough to have been copied often. Its decorative pattern of Murano glass is composed of four different colours, each in four different sizes. The pattern is quite deliberate although it is intentionally irregular, based on pictorial motifs by Paul Klee. It gives the feeling of a moving surface, as if it were permanently under water.

The stairway to the mezzanine level

1961–1963 ▸ Gavina Showroom
Via Altabella, Bologna

Opposite page:
View of the office with the table designed by Carlo Scarpa, model name: Doge

Right:
The façade made of striped concrete with openings for display windows

This shop, on the ground floor of a Bologna house, was previously an ironmonger's. Scarpa had to reshape an untidy space fragmented by load-bearing walls and unsuited to the client's display purposes.

Carlo Scarpa first set up a sort of shield, a large concrete slab chiselled in long strips and rhythmically structured by gilded stripes and by three openings, a double ring, a single ring, and the entrance in the middle. The glass of the display windows, flush with the front of the building, is held by bronze and cast-iron fittings.

Scarpa was always meticulous about thresholds. The theme of crossing over from one place to another was for him an inexhaustible source of invention. One can only speak of architecture when there is a clearly delimited area, a boundary between two units; that is what makes an awareness of transition, of passage, so important.

Here Scarpa planned a small anteroom closed by a modestly dimensioned but elegant lattice door. It separates the inside from the outside and invites people to come in, but does not shut off the interior from the outside world. It has steel sections carrying walnut wood battens. After passing through the little anteroom one passes by a revolving door into the shop. This door, built of Japanese fir, padauk wood and glass, allows the shop area to be seen before it is entered.

Scarpa exploited the vertical structural elements in the display rooms and, by exaggerating their size, converted them into plastic, coloured features of the spatial composition. Their materials include rough plaster, wood, black laminate, cobalt blue or brilliant white stucco with a silver coating. The brown synthetic flooring is separated from the wall by a stone gutter. The walls were lime-washed. Instead of reducing the structural parts to a visual minimum, Scarpa exaggerated them. They almost lose their structural purpose and become more important as pure architecture.

Left:
The design of an interior pilaster, in the foreground the "Sanluca" chair designed by the Castiglioni Brothers

Opposite page:
Delivery door

1961–1963 ▸ Fondazione Querini-Stampalia

Santa Maria Formosa, Castello, Venice ▸ with Carlo Maschietto

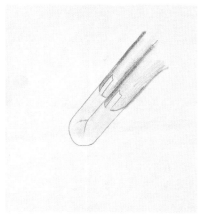

Design for the brass caps at the end of the railings for the bridge

Giuseppe Mazzariol, Carlo Scarpa's friend and colleague at the Architectural Faculty of Venice, where Mazzariol lectured on architectural history, was Director of the Querini-Stampalia Foundation in the early 1960s. When the decision to restore this sixteenth-century Venetian palace was taken, Mazzariol asked Scarpa to remodel both the ground floor, unusable because of periodic flooding, and the courtyard. The building houses exhibition rooms and the foundation's library and had been disfigured by nineteenth-century remodelling measures which were now to be reversed.

Scarpa knew that any attempt to keep water out would be destined to failure, thus he opted for a playful approach. He built a "catwalk" clad in stone and allowed the water to penetrate the building at the entrance and then to run through the rooms in a conduit along the wall in order to neutralize the effects of periodic flooding.

The entrance to the palazzo is over a bridge connecting it to the *campiello*, the little square beside the church of Santa Maria Formosa. The bridge is also typically Venetian. It is of steel, shaped like a drawn bow, and sits on blocks of Istrian stone—on one side directly at the frontage, on the other side at the street along the canal. The structure is built of two arches of sheet steel connected by massive square sections. The flat steel railing uprights are topped with a circular tube, together with a ship-style teak handrail. The railing itself is built up from three segments which, by their straightness, effectively serve to emphasize the arch shape of the little bridge. The stairs and treads are made

The "catwalk" with water flowing in from the channel and the big metal-grid in the doorway

of larch heartwood. To the left of the bridge two identical gates close the two arches of the porch facing the channel. Each gate has two parts. The upper part is made of vertical round bars of a special brass alloy fixed into an iron frame. The lower part has iron sections of different thickness arranged in an oriental pattern.

After crossing the bridge and passing through the glass-sided porch, visitors find themselves standing on the marble floor of the entrance hall, a polychrome mosaic with motifs by Paul Klee, already used by Scarpa in the Museo Castelvecchio. The wall cladding consists of white plastered light masonry, placed slightly away from the wall to ensure ventilation and protect it from dampness. The ceilings are plastered with orange-red Venetian hard plaster. From the entrance hall, one passes a ceiling-high glass wall before climbing gently to the conference and exhibition hall. The need to conceal the new heating units was achieved by using an elaborately sculptured cladding of Istrian stone.

In the large exhibition hall which extends to the courtyard, stone bands break up the exposed concrete of the plinths and floor. This floor is a modern interpretation of the traditional surfacing of stone and gravel used in the courtyards and "porteghi", or colonnades, of a Venetian palazzo. Above the plinth the walls are clad with two broad strips of travertine marble from Rapolano, separated at eye level by a brass moulding.

The two photos illustrate how the travertine door in the entrance of the palazzo opens.

Fluorescent tubes protected by frosted glass are integrated flush with the stone cladding. The integration of a door leading to a small room reserved for those attending conferences is especially successful.

The room opens on to the small, rectangular garden. Scarpa raised the garden level to create a more intimate relationship between indoors and out. One side of the garden is bounded by a concrete wall covered with a mosaic designed by Mario De Luigi, resembling that on the wall of the Brion Family Tomb.

The garden layout is Scarpa's interpretation of the traditional Venetian garden, in keeping with the regional character of the architecture. Water again has its chance. A small pool of violet marble from the Apulian Alps collects water dripping from a pipe and leads it through a maze of pools before it flows into a deep brook with water lilies. At the other end of the pool, where birds drink, the water flows over a little waterfall alongside the wall of a dried-up well. Carlo Scarpa's operation concludes with the design of the lift shaft and door and window locks, and the restoration of the stairs leading to the library on the first floor. On the landing there is a particularly interesting lamp in a Brazilian rosewood frame, carried on a polygonally carved standard. Two milk glass panes protect the bulbs.

Above and opposite page:
**Two views of the garden with water being
channelled around the sculptures, paths and
lawn areas**

1964–1974 ▸ Casa Balboni

Dorsoduro, Venice ▸ with Sergio Los, Giovanni Soccol

Opposite page:
View of the openings on the sleeping level that establish a visual connection between the two floors

Right:
View from the garden with the bay window on the right

Below:
The spiral stairway

Scarpa did not complete the reconstruction and refurbishing of this Venetian house. It is a long two-storey building, with one short side facing the Grand Canal, the other looking onto a garden. Scarpa wanted the light from the water and the garden to be exploited to the utmost as a light continuum. He therefore made use of a spiral staircase, built two openings to link the storeys visually, and chose clear light colours. On the canal side, the stairs built of Lasa marble lead to the living room, bedroom and additional rooms used by the lady of the house. Two rooms were added on the garden side of the house with a bay window and a kitchen as well as a terrace on the roof in order to increase the living space. The floors of red Lasa marble are particularly attractive. They have a profile and are separated from the walls by a gutter. The house was built by an architect named Soccol. On the whole, it is an interesting example of the renovation of an old Venetian house in an unusual location.

1965–1972 ▸ Casa de Benedetti-Bonaiuto

Rome ▸ with Federico Motterle, Carlo Maschietto, Sergio Los, E. Vittoria

This page and opposite page above:
Façade of the house in the garden of a villa from the 17th century on Via Salaria

Opposite page below:
Detail of the outside staircase and living room with fireplace on the first floor

Below:
Drawing of the layout of the raised floor level

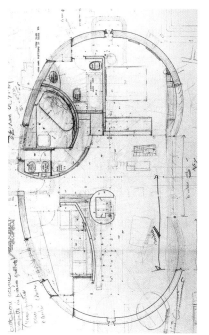

This project was intended to include the restoration of a seventeenth-century Roman villa on the Via Salaria as well as the building of a small new house in the adjacent park. Scarpa concentrated first on the new house, which he visualized as a costly étui, like a Venetian snuff box. The architect drew a pavilion supported by two walls which created an open space on the ground floor. The pavilion itself, like houses designed by Ludwig Mies van der Rohe, consists of a large open space uniformly defined in individual areas. He steadily worked away at a basic design consisting of different circles, and finally arrived at a project which reminded him of the architecture of Borromini. The support for the roof, itself a kind of shield pointing at the sky, was to have the minimum possible effect on the ground plan. Scarpa wanted to solve this problem with slim cylindrical double columns to be made out of steel.

Intended for an elderly lady, the mother of a lawyer named De Benedetti, this simple house was designed on one level. The entrance was intended to be a sort of bridge, a sloping platform between the trees.

The whole composition depended on the contrast between a pavilion, with its rounded and curved lines reminiscent of Roman Baroque, and the supporting walls which were informed by Neoplasticism.

1966–1985 ▸ Entrance to the Architectural Faculty

Venice University, Venice ▸ with Sergio Los

View of the new entrance to the campus
The sliding door, closed

During the restoration of the Venice architectural faculty in the Tolentini monastery, a gateway of Istrian stone was found. At first it was thought that it might be used as the entrance to the faculty.

When Scarpa was given the project, he did not think of this "natural" application. He did not want the gate to be used as an entrance but displayed as a museum piece. After this had finally been decided, Scarpa brushed up the symbolic content of the gate, duplicating its allusions, and placed it in a web of cross-references, charging it with meaning as he so often did with exhibits.

The wall which was to enclose the little Campo dei Tolentini in front of the faculty was also rejected by Scarpa. The solution he proposed was to separate the structural from the architectural function. The wall encloses a small courtyard from the outside, but from the inside it almost disappears and becomes a part of the ground.

Scarpa designed three entrances, the first in 1966, the second in 1972. His last project, never completed, further developed the preceding ideas, and occupied him time and again during the last two years of his life. For the entrance construction I have relied on the second draft project, which contains a number of notes, as well as drawings intended for submission to the city council.

View of the monumental door from inside

Below:
View of the campus from outside with the reflecting pool and monumental doorway

The wall to the left of the entrance contains the gate and supports a broad canopy to protect people from the rain while awaiting admission. The gate is like a pair of scales in unstable equilibrium balanced on a wheel. One side consists of a heavy slab of Istrian stone bearing a quotation from Vico *"verum ipsum factum"*. The other side closes the entrance with a steel-framed glass sheet. A second wheel balances the gate and adjusts its movement.

The ancient gateway lies in the pool of water surrounded by steps that lead towards the edges of the pool and the water's surface, creating a vibrant, relief-like underwater landscape.

The gate thus becomes a metaphor for an entrance, consciously detached from the role that functionalism would accord it. It is a lesson in architecture that makes critical use of the discipline's own language.

1968–1983 ▸ Fondazione Masieri

Dorsoduro, Venice ▸ with Carlo Maschietto, Franca Semi

The access way to the rooms with the curved walls of the bathrooms
The double-columned, steel structure is independent of the walls.

The chequered history of the Masieri Foundation building, now a *Galleria di Architettura*, dates from Scarpa's cooperation with the young Friulian architect Angelo Masieri, who, like Scarpa, believed that architecture should follow Frank Lloyd Wright. Some projects from these years, for example the bank at Tarvisio and a villa at Cervignano, illustrate their joint search for the new concept of space which characterized organic architecture at the time.

Angelo Masieri died after a car accident in the USA in 1952. In his memory, his parents commissioned Frank Lloyd Wright, whom he had never met, to renovate a building they owned on the Grand Canal in Venice, where they intended to establish a foundation under the aegis of the Istituto Universitario di Architettura di Venezia.

Wright's project aroused furious controversy and no one dared to take it up. Scarpa's hopes that planning consent might after all be granted a few years later were not realized. In 1962 the Foundation commissioned Valeriano Pastor to draw up a new plan with strict instructions on the conservation of the existing structure, but without success. So it was left to Scarpa to investigate the possibilities of converting the building into a students' hostel. Between 1968 and 1969 he put forward various draft proposals, but they met with resistance, particularly because of the façade overlooking the Grand Canal. Finally Scarpa discovered a drawing by Canaletto showing a façade with two chimneys, which predated the existing one. In collaboration with an engineer named Maschietto, he developed a steel structure that was independent of its cladding to minimize the thickness of the interim floors from which the façade is suspended, although they appear to be separate from it. In 1973 the project was finally approved.

After Scarpa's death the building remained a half-finished skeleton until his former collaborator, Carlo Maschietto, and the architect Franca Semi completed it in 1983.

Opposite page:
The stairway that connects the different levels from the ground floor up
In the ceiling and the floor the steel members are visible.

1969–1978 ▸ Brion Family Tomb

San Vito d'Altivole, Treviso ▸ with Guido Pietropoli, Carlo Maschietto

Opposite page:

During the funeral ceremonies the double door in front of the altar can be opened. The reflecting pool on the other side ensures good light inside.

Right:

View of the Brion Family Tomb at the municipal cemetery

Below:

Design for the altar

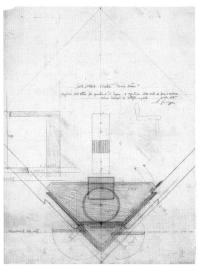

"Someone died, here in Italy, and the family wanted to commemorate the achievements of this person who came from a humble background—*dalla gavetta* as we say—and who, through his work, attained a certain importance ... In fact a mere 100 square metres would have sufficed but I was given 2,200 square metres ... Well, I did what you have seen. The monument or the sarcophagi to stand here on a prominent site, with a panorama. The deceased wanted to be close to the earth of the village where he was born, so I had the idea of building a small arch which I call the *arcosolium*, a Latin term used by the early Christians. In the catacombs, important people or martyrs were given a more lavish tomb, called an *arcosolium*, but here I chose a simple arch.

It is beautiful when two people who have loved each other in life continue to bow in mutual greeting in death. They should not be erect: that would be for soldiers. So an arch was built, a bridge made of reinforced concrete. But, to take away the impression of a bridge, the arch had to be decorated, the vault painted. I covered my arch in mosaic, a Venetian tradition which I interpreted in my own way.

The great cypress avenue leading to the graveyard is an Italian tradition, it is a sort of racetrack, a wide, long road. Architects have had enough of these racetracks. This

Left:
Access way to the chapel from the street

Below:
View and cross section of the chapel from the northwest

Opposite page, above:
Final design for the Brion Family Tomb

Opposite page, below:
Corner of the portico decorated with mosaic tiles

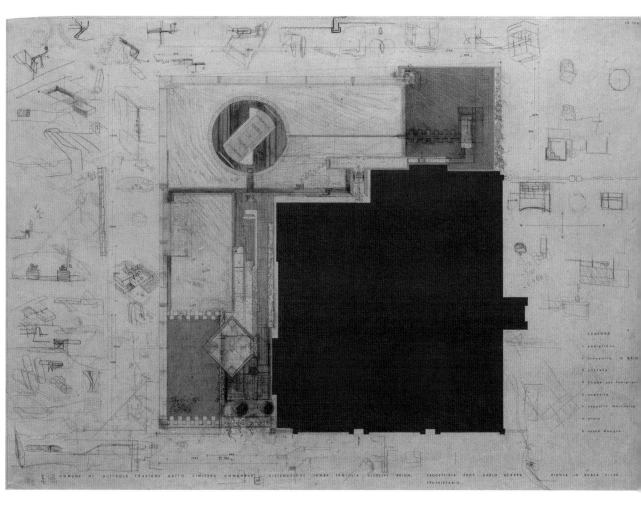

road is called the *propylaeum* after the Greek word for entrance, and that is the 'portico', a colonnade. This is the starting point. These two eyes determine the view. The site was just too large; it gave the feeling of a meadow. To justify the large area it seemed sensible to me to build a little temple for funeral services-'burial' is such a terrible word.

But the area was still too large, so we raised the ground level to be able to see outside. So one can look out but nothing can be seen from outside. Here are the tombstones, the graves of the family, the little temple, the altar.

From the village, the site is approached through a private entrance; here is the church, where funeral services are held, the village cemetery, and here is the chapel—this is accessible to the public because the ground belongs to the estate. Only the family has the right to be buried there. A private path leads to the little pavilion on the water—the only really private area on the site. That is basically all there is.

This place of the dead is a little like a garden. Incidentally, the great American cemeteries of the nineteenth century, in Chicago, for example, are extensive parks. No Napoleonic mausoleum, no! You can drive in with your car. There are beautiful monuments, for example those by Louis Henry Sullivan. Cemeteries now have become mere

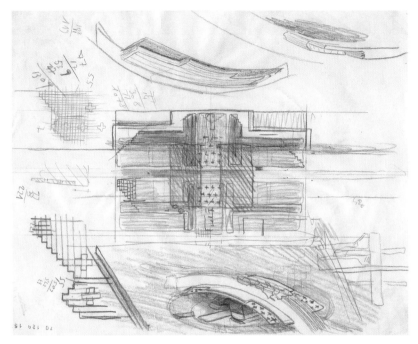

piles of shoeboxes, stacked mechanically one on top of the other. I wanted to express the naturalness of water and meadow, of water and earth. Water is the source of life."

Apart from the fact that the description by Scarpa quoted at length here explains his motives and preferences as an architect, it reminds those who knew him of his ironical way of speaking about architecture. His lectures were charming conversations quite devoid of any academic tone. Carlo Scarpa designed the Brion tomb during the student revolt in Italian universities. Architecture was forgotten, politically irrelevant. Scarpa was director of the Venice faculty, an institute which no one at the time wanted to run. But his friendly manner disarmed the ubiquitous aggressiveness of the demagogues.

The L-shaped site is situated along two sides of the cemetery of San Vito d'Altivole near Asolo. A boundary wall leaning inwards encloses the site with its three centres: the pool around the pavilion, the *arcosolium* at the corner of the "L", and the chapel. There are two entrances, one directly from outside to the chapel, the other from the cemetery at the end of the main avenue. This second entrance gives access to the site; Scarpa borrowed the name *propylaeum* from the Acropolis. It leads to a portico, from which one sees the garden through two intersecting mosaic-framed rings.

To the right the visitor sees the only area closed to the public—the pavilion of meditation surrounded by a pool. Its glass access door is operated by counterweights and rollers visible from outside. Between the water lilies in the pool an emblem can be seen, a cruciform maze.

The interlocking circles of the portico

A corner of the surrounding wall seen from inside

The water is led off into a little brook that ends near the tombs. At a lower level, over-hung by the *arcosolium*, are two gravestones of light and dark stone, each of which sup-ports a jacaranda wood sarcophagus in which the letters of the names are inscribed in ebony and ivory. Off to the side, in the meadow, the graves of the family are located under a roof, which seems almost to float despite its apparent weight.

At the end of the garden we come to the chapel, which is directly connected to the cemetery drive via an iron-framed concrete gate. The chapel is rectangular, set in plan at 45 degrees to the enclosing wall, and dominated by a stepped motif. Surrounded by water and cypress trees, this is the last episode of a place with an oriental yet deeply Venetian atmosphere, where one would gladly see children playing on the grass.

Nothing disturbs the evocative intensity of the pure architecture. In a corner of the garden, a tomb designed by Carlo Scarpa's son, Tobia, is a reminder that the architect is buried here.

Above:
**View of the *arcosolium* from the south with
the channel that runs from the pond, along
the portico entrance to the cemetery**

Right:
**The two sarcophagi under the *arcosolium* are
inclined towards each other.**

Opposite page:
**View of the western corner of the chapel
surrounded by a channel of water**

1973–1982 ▸ Banca Popolare di Verona
Piazza Nogara, Verona ▸ with Arrigo Rudi

Carlo Scarpa's new building of the Banca Popolare di Verona is on the site of two demolished buildings next to the existing bank, which is still in use. The project underwent
many changes over the years both as a result of the client's new specifications and of
the architect's fresh thoughts. Continual revision and critical examination, which often
led to imperceptible modifications, were important to his method of working. This
"filing down" was a process of small corrections leading to the final shape of the whole
project; according to Scarpa, just like a woman's face, which would lose its charisma
and harmony were but a slight change made to its proportions or to a single detail.

The main themes of the project did not change: a forward-thrusting front elevation,
constructed on the classical three principles of plinth, middle part and cornice. Originally the rear elevation was provided with continuous horizontal bands, unlike the front,
but the two are now basically similar.

When Carlo Scarpa suddenly died in November 1978, the building was largely complete. The front and rear elevations facing the Piazza and the courtyard had been built,
and much of the material for interior fittings ordered. Arrigo Rudi, who had worked on

Access door to the first floor

the project throughout, including its construction, saw it through to a successful conclusion.

The façade is one of the most interesting elements of the building. The window-panes either are deeply recessed or project well-beyond the openings. This basic theme is echoed in the elements made of rough-sawn oak as well as in the bay windows that project from the façade like crystal shrines. The circular windows have different diameters, a trick used by Scarpa to achieve liveliness.

The plinth is of Botticino marble, as is the cornice. Classical motifs are quoted in its stepped cross section. Scarpa built up this section from two courses of blocks laid one above the other. One course is set back, on the one hand to emphasize the difference between them, and on the other to keep water out. The cornice is reminiscent of crowning elements on Venetian palazzi; in particular the idea of projecting surfaces on which a strong light falls was inspired mainly by elements such as those at the Fondaco dei Turchi in Venice. A red Verona marble cornice with dogtooth moulding also appears on both façades as well as over the windows and, inside, on the staircase.

The main surfaces of the façades terminate at the level of the top-floor windows, as if the bank's flat roof were floating above them. In the loggia above, the materials are different, with metal beams and columns and a frieze of coloured mosaic. The long

Southern view of the stairway which consists of a grid of steel pipes connected by bronze angles and encased in reinforced concrete. It supports the glazing on the eastern side of the building.

Rear façade

View of the wood-panelled connector between the existing and the new buildings

The lift with its curved, red wall connects the offices of the directors on the first floor with the second floor.

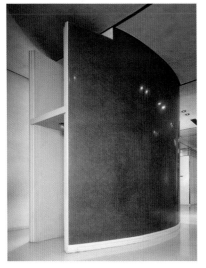

strip of the main beam, made of two steel joists of different sizes connected by bolts and gussets, is supported at regular intervals by pairs of thin cylindrical steel columns. These double cylinders are held top and bottom by a link of Muntz metal, a brass with a high zinc content.

Inside the building, the tall, polygonal columns are reinforced with concrete with a cylindrical metal plinth and a band of gold around the capital. These columns give continuity to the internal space with its different events at different levels. This is also helped by the arrangement of the walls and by the unifying effect of openings on the different levels.

The glazed external stairway in the back is constructed of reinforced concrete and is plastered with mortar made of slaked lime and marble. The inside of the staircase is a "cage" of steel tubing with rectangular bronze joints. The stairs are made of corrosion-resistant concrete with an iron grid at the core.

In this context, the staff staircase is interesting—two parallel separate flights which provide continuity in the vertical direction. The edges are protected by brass rails. The walls are covered with polished green and violet Venetian hard plaster.

The service stairway connects the ground floor with the office level.

Detail of the service stairway

Across the courtyard, where Scarpa originally proposed a garden, is a roofed steel footbridge, about 20 metres long, clad with curved copper-plated plywood sheets.

The Banca Popolare di Verona is an example of Scarpa's ability to introduce a new building into a historic city without historicist imitation, but rather in lively dialogue with the existing context.

1974–1979 ‣ Casa Ottolenghi

Bardolino, Verona ‣ with Giuseppe Tommasi, Carlo Maschietto, Guido Pietropoli

Opposite page:
View from the south of the courtyard on the east side of the house with a pond into which the rainwater collected on the upper floor runs

Passageway to the living room with the fireplace in blue and bright yellow by Mario De Luigi

In 1974 a lawyer named Ottolenghi commissioned Scarpa to build him a house on Lake Garda in the village of Mure, near Bardolino. Planning regulations allowed no more than one storey above ground level. As often happens, this restriction became an important element of the architectural design. The solution was a building partly sunk into the earth and organized round nine circular columns which determine the arrangement of the rooms. The house is scarcely distinguishable from the natural surroundings in which it is half immersed. The roof became, in Carlo Scarpa's own words, "an area of rough ground which can be walked on".

The reinforced concrete structure forms a roof of slanted surfaces clad in brick outside and covered with polished, black plaster inside. The ceiling reflects the surrounding landscape with columns to which the trilithic principle was applied, although not in the conventional manner, but nevertheless evoked. The columns affect the roofed courtyard, by deforming it. Light and air come into the building via a passageway called a "calle", which separates it from the encompassing wall. The result is the conjunction of two curved surfaces, one of which, as Giuseppe Tommasi explains, is "conical, while the other joins up with a rectangular segment, an encompassing arch with vertical surface lines."

The most important elements of the design are the massive columns made of layers of concrete and rough-cut stone. Carlo Scarpa wanted the stone to be cut while building was in progress, but it was not technically possible to process stone and concrete at the same time. The stone first chosen was local limestone from Prun, but it was then decided to add a few layers of Trani stone to refine the colour balance. Thick

The fireplace on the southeast wall of the main bedroom

columns are also found in other designs by Scarpa, for example for the Villa Zoppas at Conegliano and the cinema at Valdobbiadene, or the Casa Roth at Asolo, but only here did he actually build them. As pivotal points in a polygonal organization of space, the columns connect various areas in an unusual geometric structure. If we were not aware that Scarpa avoided representational shapes, we could see in this project a forerunner of the compositional experiments of deconstructivism.

The interference between tradition and invention also inspired the idea for a concrete floor, cast and then polished, containing pieces of ceramic tiles and small coloured stones to create a pattern anticipating or guiding any possible crack-lines.

Of the elements that serve to structure the interior, the fireplace, the Calacata marble and the vibrantly colourful plaster in the bathroom, executed by Eugenio de Luigi, are particularly notable. The bathroom thereby becomes a central element. Its form is defined by the intersection of two circles-a motif often found in Scarpa's architecture. This bathroom serves as a division between the bedroom and the large living room. Scarpa's idea was for reflecting glass to enable those in the bathroom to see out without themselves being seen. The occupant of the bathroom feels he is in an exten-

The building element containing the bathroom for the master bedroom with a large, glass opening
The mirrored glass allows for a view out while preventing people from seeing inside.

sion of the living room. By contrast, the interior of the bathroom is invisible from the living room. The interior furnishings were also designed by the architect, including the "Cornaro" sofa and the "Scarpi" table.

Life and Work

Nini Scarpa at the Royal Institute of British Architects, London, on the occasion of preparations for a show of her husband's work, 1974

1906 ▶ Carlo Scarpa is born on June 2 in Venice to the elementary school teacher Antonio Scarpa and Emma Novello.

1908 ▶ The family moves to Vicenza.

1919 ▶ After the mother's death the family returns to Venice. Carlo attempts in vain to enter the Academy of Fine Art.

1920 ▶ Scarpa is accepted at the Accademia Reale di Belle Arti.

1922 ▶ As a student, he works for two years in Vincenzo Rinaldo's architectural office.

1924
Annex to Villa Gioacchino Velluti, Dolo, Venice

1926 ▶ Scarpa receives his diploma of architectural drawing and becomes a teaching assistant to Professor Guido Girilli at the Venice architectural faculty.
Restoration of Villa Angelo Velo in collaboration with Franco Pizzuto, Fontaniva, Padua
Construction plans for building the Villa Angelo Velo in collaboration with Franco Pizzuto, Fontaniva, Padua
Construction of a residential ensemble in collaboration with Franco Pizzuto, Fontaniva, Padua
Villa Giovanni Campagnolo in collaboration with Franco Pizzuto, Fontaniva, Padua
Villa Aldo Martinati in collaboration with Franco Pizzuto, Padua

1927 ▶ In addition to his teaching, Scarpa opens his own office and works as an artistic adviser to the Cappellin glass factory until 1930.

1928
Interior of the Cappellin glassware shop, Florence

1929
Interior decoration and furnishings for Villa Vittorio Donà, Murano, Venice

1930 ▶ German architectural journals draw his attention to the work of Ludwig Mies van der Rohe and Frank Lloyd Wright.

1931
Renovation of Café Lavena, Frezzeria, Venice
Living room of the Pelzel home, Murano, Venice
Interior decoration and furnishings for the home of Ferruccio Asta, Venice

1932
Renovation of the Sfriso silverware shop, Campo San Tomà, Venice
Collaboration with Mario De Luigi on the fresco mosaic Il bagno, 18th Venice Biennale

1933 ▶ Scarpa becomes a lecturer at the Venice architectural faculty and begins his work for the Venini glass factory on Murano—a cooperation which lasts over 14 years.

1934 ▶ Carlo Scarpa marries Onorina Lazzari, granddaughter of the architect Vincenzo Rinaldo, for whom he worked as a student.

1935 ▶ His son Tobia is born.
Interior decoration and design for the Society of Decorative Arts of Venice

1936
Restoration and renovation of Ca' Foscari, Faculty of Economics, University of Venice
Interior design for the Casino of Venice Lido
Stand for the Venini Company, Murano, at the 6th Milan Triennale

1937
Design of the exhibition: Oreficeria Veneziana, Loggetta dei Sansovino, Venice
Renovation of the Teatro Rossini, Venice
1939 Interiors of the Flavio Perfumery and Beauty Parlour, Venice Lido

1940
Tomb of Vettore Rizzo, San Michele Cemetery, Venice
Venini stand at the 7th Milan Triennale

1941
Renovation of the home of Gino Sacerdoti, Santa Maria del Giglio, Venice
Plan for the Il Cavallino Art Gallery, Riva degli Schiavoni, Venice

Opposite page:
Carlo Scarpa in the early 1970s

Carlo Scarpa and Sergio Los, 1967

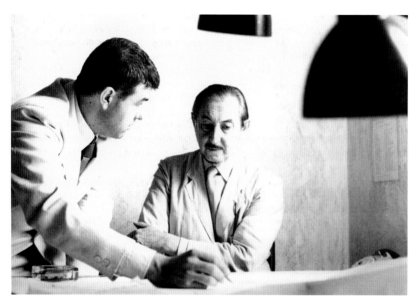

Furnishing for the home of Arturo Martini, San Gregorio, Venice
Bedroom and dining room furniture for Gigi Scarpa, Venice

1942 ▶ Together with the artist Mario De Luigi, Scarpa accepts his first design contract for the Venice Biennale, to which he will contribute for 30 years.
Plan and interiors for the Pellizzari home, Venice
Design of the exhibition: Arturo Martini in collaboration with Mario De Luigi
Central Pavilion of the Biennale, Castello Gardens, Venice

1943
Tomb of the Capovilla Family, San Michele Cemetery, Venice

1944
Interiors for the Tessiladriatica shop, Campo Santi Apostoli, Venice
Renovation of Bellotto home, Campo Santi Apostoli, Venice

1945
Restoration of the Gallerie dell'Accademia, Venice

1947
Banca Cattolica del Veneto, Tarvisio, Udine, in collaboration with Angelo Masieri; completed by Masieri in 1949
Collaboration with Angelo Masieri on the Villa Giacomuzzi, Udine

1948
Exhibit designs for the 24th Venice Biennale, Castello Gardens, Venice
Design for the First Exhibition of Film Technology, temporary cinema pavilion, Venice Lido
Restoration of the Pedrocchi Café, Padua

1949
Interior design for the new section of Il Cavallino Art Gallery, Piscina di Frezzeria, Venice
Stand for the Press and Cinema Advertising, temporary cinema pavilion, Venice Lido
Design of the exhibition: Giovanni Bellini, Venice
Design of the exhibition: Show of comtemporary Art, Ala Napoleonica, Venice

1950
Collaboration with Angelo Masieri on the Casa Bortolotto, Cervignano del Friuli, Udine
Design of TELVE public telephone centre, Venice

Layout and furnishings for Ferdinando Ongania's antique shop, Bocca di Piazza, Venice
Interior design for the A la piavola de Franza clothing shop, Bocca di Piazza, Venice
Book Pavilion at the Biennale, Castello Gardens, Venice
Exhibit designs for the 25th Biennale, Castello Gardens, Venice
Installations for the exhibition: Posters of the Biennale, 25th Biennale, Ala Napoleonica, Venice
Design of the exhibition: Images of Work in Contemporary Painting, Ala Napoleonica, Venice
Installations for the exhibition: Cinema Books and Periodicals, 25th Biennale, Palazzo del Cinema, Venice Lido

1951 ▶ Scarpa meets Frank Lloyd Wright in Venice.
Collaboration with Angelo Masieri on the Veritti Tomb, Udine
Design of the exhibition: Giambatista Tiepolo, Castello Gardens, Venice

1952
Garden design for the Villa Guarnieri, Venice Lido
Exhibit designs for the 26th Biennale, Castello Gardens, Venice
Design of the exhibition: Toulouse-Lautrec, Venice
Installation of an exhibition for the Istituto Nazionale di Urbanistica conference, Ca' Giustinian, Venice
Installation of an exhibition of historical financial documents from the Commune of Siena, Marciana library, Venice
Renovation of the Ambrosini home, Venice

1953
Renovation of the historic sections of the Correr Museum, Venice
Design of the exhibition: Antonello da Messina and the Quattrocento in Sicily, Palazzo del Municipio, Messina
Restoration of Palazzo Abatellis as the Galleria Nazionale di Sicilia, Palermo
Design for the Villa Zoppas, Conegliano, Treviso

1954 ▶ On the invitation of the Italian-American Association for Cultural Relations, Scarpa lectures

in Rome; one of his subjects is museum design.
*Design of the exhibition: Arte antica cinese,
Doge's Palace, Venice*
*Design for the first six halls at the Uffizi gallery,
Florence, in collaboration with Ignazio Gardella
and Giovanni Michelucci*
*Venezuela Pavilion at the Biennale, Castello
Gardens, Venice*

1955 ▸ Important architects propose that Scarpa
be awarded an honorary doctorate.
*Installation of Leoncillo Leoncilli's statue La
partigiana, Castello Gardens, Venice*
*Interior design for the Manlio Capitolo Civil
Court, Venice*
*Interior design for the law office and home of the
lawyer Scatturin, Venice*
*Interior design of the Council Chamber of the
Amministrazione Provinciale, Parma*
*Renovation of the Aula magna of Ca' Foscari,
University of Venice*
*Extension of the Gipsoteca Canoviana, Possagno,
Treviso*
Casa Veritti, Udine

1956 ▸ Scarpa has to defend himself in court
against the accusation by the Venice Association
of Architects that he is working as an architect
without the necessary education or licence. He is
acquitted. Also in 1956, with Ludovico Quaroni he
is awarded the Olivetti Prize for Architecture.
*Collaboration with Edoardo Detti on a parish
church, Fiorenzuola*
*Design of the exhibition: Piet Mondrian, Valle
Giulia Modern Art Gallery, Rome*
*Restoration and exhibit design of the Museo
Castelvecchio, Verona*

1957
Plan for a campsite, Fusina, Venice
*Design for the Casa Taddei, Rio Terà dei
Catecumeni, Venice*
Olivetti Showroom, Procuratie Vecchie, Venice
*Renovation of the Quadreria at the Correr
Museum, Venice*
*Collaboration with Edoardo Detti on the plan for
the renovation of the drawings and prints
collection in the Uffizi Gallery, Florence*

1958
*Exhibit designs for the 29th Biennale, Castello
Gardens, Venice*
*Design of the exhibition: Da Altichiero a
Pisanello, Museo Castelvecchio, Verona*
*Collaboration with Carlo Maschietto on a high
school in Chioggia, Venice*

1959
*Collaboration with Edoardo Gellner on the ENI
village church, Borca di Cadore*
*Design of the exhibition: Vitalità nell'arte,
Palazzo Grassi, Venice*
*Design of the exhibition: Vetri di Murano dal
1860 al 1960, Gran Guardia, Verona*
*Renovation of the Taddei home, Palazzo
Morosini, Venice*

1960
Plan for the D'Ambrogio home, Udine
Interior design of the Villa Scatturin, Venice
Salviati Glassware showroom, Venice
Zilio Tomb, Udine Cemetery
*Design of the exhibition: Frank Lloyd Wright,
12th Triennale, Milan*
*Exhibit designs for the 30th Biennale, Castello
Gardens, Venice*

1961
*Design of the exhibition: Il senso dei colore e il
dominio delle acque in the Veneto Pavilion at the
Italia '61 national exhibition, Turin*
*Renovation of the ground floor and courtyard of
the Fondazione Querini-Stampalia, Venice*
Gavina Showroom, Bologna

1962 ▸ Scarpa becomes a full Professor of
Interior Design and moves to Asolo, Treviso.
*Exhibit designs for the 31st Biennale, Castello
Gardens, Venice*
*Design of the exhibition: Cima da Conegliano,
Palazzo dei Trecento, Treviso*
Interior design for the Villa Gallo, Vicenza

1963
*Design for the Casa Cassina, Ronco di Carimate,
Como*

1964
Restoration of the Villa Balboni, Venice
*Exhibit designs for the 32nd Biennale, Castello
Gardens, Venice*
*Design of the exhibition: Giacomo Manzù, Ala
Napoleonica, Venice*
Renovation of the Zentner House, Zurich

1965 ▸ He is awarded the IN-ARCH Prize and the
Gold Medal for Art and Culture by the Ministry of
Education in Rome for his renovation of the
Museo Castelvecchio.
Villa De Benedetti-Bonaiuto, Rome; not finished

1966
*Exhibit designs for the 33rd Biennale, central
pavilion, Castello Gardens, Venice*
*Design for the La poesia section at the Expo '67
in Montreal*

1967 ▸ Scarpa travels to the USA to see buildings
by Frank Lloyd Wright. He meets Louis Kahn.
*Design of the exhibition: Arturo Martini,
Santa Caterina, Treviso*

1968
*Installation of the new Monument to Partisan
Women by Augusto Murer, Venice*
*Exhibit designs for the 34th Biennale, central
pavilion, Castello Gardens, Venice*
Fondazione Masieri, Venice

1969
*Design of the exhibition: Affreschi fiorentini,
Hayward Gallery, London*
Brion Family Tomb, San Vito d'Altivole, Treviso
*Design of the exhibition: Erich Mendelsohn
Drawings, University of California, Berkeley*

1970
*Design of the exhibition: Giorgio Morandi, Royal
Academy of Arts, London*

1972 ▸ Scarpa becomes the head of the architec-
tural faculty. He moves with his office to Vicenza.
*Design of the exhibition: Capolavori della pittura
dei XX secolo, Ala Napoleonica, Venice*
*Exhibit designs for the 36th Biennale, Castello
Gardens, Venice*

Scarpa and his son Tobia at the Fondazione Querini-Stampalia in Venice in the early 1960s

Renovation of the Franchetti Gallery, Ca' d'Oro, Venice

1973
Design of the exhibition: Le Corbusier purista e il progretto di Pessac, Fondazione Querini Stampalia, Venice
Banca Popolare di Verona, Verona; completed after Scarpa's death by Arrigo Rudi

1974
Apartment block, Vicenza
Design of the exhibition: Venice and Byzantium, Doge's Palace, Venice
Design of the exhibition: Gino Rossi, Ca' da Noal, Treviso
Design of the exhibition: Carlo Scarpa, Heinz Gallery, London
Design of the exhibition: Carlo Scarpa, Domus Comestabilis, Vicenza

External renovation of the Villa Palazzetto, Monselice, Padua
Modification and extension of the San Sebastiano Convent for the new premises of the Faculty of Literature and Philosophy, University of Venice; completed by Guido Pietropoli, 1979
Casa Ottolenghi, Bardolino, Verona

1975
Renovation of the Aula Magna at the Istituto Universitario di Architettura, Venice
Design of the exhibition: Giuseppe Samonà, Palazzo Grassi, Venice
Design of the exhibition: Carlo Scarpa at the Institut de l'Environnement, Paris

1976
Commemorative stele to the victims of the terrorist massacre in Piazza della Loggia, Brescia
Doorway of the San Sebastiano Convent, Venice

1977
Collaboration with Roberto Calandra on the plan of Palazzo Chiaromonte as offices for the dean and the museum of Palermo University
Interior design for a flat, Montecchio, Vicenza
Design of the exhibition: Alberto Viani, Ca' Pesaro, Venice
Zoppi flat, Vicenza

1978 ▸ Carlo Scarpa dies in Sendai during a visit to Japan on November 28. His will stipulates his burial in the Brion Family Tomb at San Vito d'Altivole. Shortly before his death, the Venice Architectural Faculty awards him an honorary doctorate.
Altar and paving for the Church of Torresino, Padua
Tomb of the Galli Family, Genoa Nervi Cemetery; executed after Scarpa's death
Design of the exhibition: Carlo Scarpa, Madrid
Design of the exhibition: Mario Cavaglieri, Accademia dei Concordi, Rovigo

Map

Bologna
Gavina Showroom

Como
Casa Cassina

Conegliano, Treviso
Villa Zoppas

Palermo
Galleria Regionale di Sicilia

Possagno, Treviso
Gipsoteca Canoviana

Rome
Casa de Benedetti-Bonaiuto

San Vito d'Altivole, Treviso
Brion Family Tomb

Udine
Casa Veritti

Venice
Casa Balboni
Entrance to the Architectural Faculty
Fondazione Masieri
Fondazione Querini-Stampalia
Museo Correr
Olivetti Showroom

Verona
Banca Popolare di Verona
Casa Ottolenghi
Museo di Castelvecchio

Bibliography

► Albertini, Bianca, Bagnoli, Sandro. *Scarpa. L'architettura del dettaglio*. Milan, 1988.

► Albertini, Bianca, Bagnoli, Sandro. *Scarpa. I musei e le esposizioni*. Milan, 1992.

► Beltramini, Guido, Forster, Kurt W., Marini, Paola (eds.). *Carlo Scarpa. Mostre e musei 1944–1976 / Case e paesaggi 1972–1978*. Milan, 2000.

► Beltramini, Guido, Zannier, Italo (eds.). *Carlo Scarpa. Atlante delle architetture*. Venice, 2006.

► Bettini, Sergio. "L'architettura di Carlo Scarpa", *Zodiac 6*, 1960.

► Brusatin, Manlio. "Carlo Scarpa Architetti Venezia", *Centro Spazio IV*, 3–4 March–April 1972.

► "Carlo Scarpa", *A+U Architecture and Urbanism*, special edition 10, 1985.

► "Carlo Scarpa Selected Drawings", *GA Document 21*, September 1988.

► Crippa, Maria Antonietta. *Scarpa: il pensiero, il disegno, di progetti*. Milan, 1984.

► Dal Co, Francesco, Mazzariol, Giuseppe. *Carlo Scarpa. Opera completa*. Milan, 1984.

► Dal Co, Francesco. *Villa Ottolenghi. Carlo Scarpa*. New York, 1998.

► Duboy, Philippe. "Carlo Scarpa", *Les cahiers de la recherche architecturale 19*, 2 Term 1986.

► Lanzarini, Orietta. *Carlo Scarpa. L'architetto e le arti Venice*, 2003.

► Los, Sergio. *Carlo Scarpa architetto poeta*. Venice, 1967.

► Los, Sergio. "Zwei Restaurierungen von Carlo Scarpa", *Werk 7*, 1969.

► Los, Sergio, Frahm, Klaus (photos). *Carlo Scarpa*. Cologne, 1993.

► Los, Sergio. *Carlo Scarpa. Guida all'architettura*. Venice, 1995.

► Los, Sergio. "Carlo Scarpa Architect and Poet", *Path, Architecture, Design, Art 2*, 2001.

► Magagnato, Licisco (ed.), Marinelli, Sergio, Dalai Emiliani, Marisa, Rudi, Arrigo. *Carlo Scarpa a Castelvecchio*. Milan, 1982.

► Magnago Lampugnani, Vittorio. *Carlo Scarpa. Architektur*. Stuttgart, 1986.

► Manzelle, Maura (ed.). *Carlo Scarpa. L'opera e la sua conservazione, Giornate di studio alla Fondazione Querini Stampalia*. Venice, 2003.

► Marcianò, Ada Francesca (ed.). *Carlo Scarpa*, Bologna, 1984.

► Mateo, Josep Lluís (ed.). *Quaderns d'arquitectura i urbanisme*. Special issue dedicated to Carlo Scarpa, Number 158, July, August, September 1983.

► Murphy, Richard. *Carlo Scarpa & Castelvecchio*. Venice, 1991.

► Noever, Peter. *The Other City. Carlo Scarpa. Die andere Stadt*. Vienna, 1989.

► Noever, Peter (ed.). *Carlo Scarpa. Das Handwerk der Architektur*. Vienna, 2003.

► Olsberg, Nicholas, Ranalli, George, Bédard, Jean-François, Polano, Sergio, Di Lieto, Alba, Fonatti, Franco. *Elemente des Bauens bei Carlo Scarpa*. Vienna, 1984.

► Friedman, Mildred, Guidi, Guido (photos). *Carlo Scarpa. Architect: Intervening with History*. New York, 1999.

► Pierconti, J. K. Mauro. *Carlo Scarpa e il Giappone*. Milan, 2007.

► Polano, Sergio. *Carlo Scarpa: Palazzo Abatellis. La Galleria della Sicilia. Palermo 1953–1954*. Milan, 1989.

► Rudi, Arrigo, Fenaroli, Francesca (ed.). "Carlo Scarpa. Frammenti 1926/1978", *Rassegna III*, 7, July 1981.

► Schultz, Anne-Catrin. *Carlo Scarpa Layers*. Stuttgart, 2007.

► Yokoyama, Tadashi, Toyota, Hiroyuki. "Carlo Scarpa", *Space Design 6*, 1977.

Credits

The Author

Sergio Los teaches Architectural Design at the University of Venice. He worked for Carlo Scarpa, also serving as his teaching assistant from 1964–1970, and has published several books about him. In 1964 he opened his first office, which later gave rise to SYNERGIA progetti srl in 1983. Working together with the architect Natasha F. Pulitzer, he has realized numerous buildings and city planning projects. His architecture appeals to the senses on a number of levels. It is regionally rooted, while also taking environmental and energy questions into consideration. Sergio Los, the author of numerous publications translated into a wide range of languages, has served as a guest lecturer at many Italian and foreign universities. His awards include the Premio Eurosolar (Berlin 2003), the WREN Pioneer Award (Florence 1998) and, together with Natasha F. Pulitzer, the PLEA (Louvain-la-Neuve 1996).